The
Runaway
and other stories

edited by
Antonio D'Amour

Written by
Antonio D'Amour
Ludger D'Amour
Roméo D'Amour
Donna D'Amour

Zenobi Publishing
North Sydney NS

Library and Archives Canada Cataloguing in Publication

The runaway and other stories \ edited by Antonio D'Amour \ written by Antonio D'Amour ... [et al.].

ISBN 0-9736830-0-7

1.   D'Amour family—Anecdotes. 2 D'Amour, Antonio, 1932—Anecdotes. D'Amour, Antonio 1932—Family—Anecdotes. I. D'Amour, Antonio, 1932-

FC27.D24R85 2004   C818'.603   C2004-905654-9

Previously Published
The following stories have been previously published:
- *The Wreck of the Alice Mae* was published in The Cape Bretoner, the NB Reader (Telegraph-Journal), Le Sanglier.
- *General Cambronne,* was published as *Discipline* in the NB Reader.
- *Man Overboard, The Dream, The Main Event, How I Discovered Electricity, The Lumberjack, Maurice Gets a Car* were also published in the NB Reader (Telegraph-Journal).
- *A Secondary Education* was published in the Antigonish Casket.
- *The Lure of the Maggies* was published in FiftyPlus.

Zenobi Publishing
37 Emerald Street
North Sydney, Nova Scotia B2A 3J8

Book layout: Gail Jones
Printed in Canada by City Printers, Sydney, NS

Dedication

To my parents Antoine D'Amour and Graziella
Turbide and all my siblings: Cyrille, Geneviève,
Roméo, Léola, Ludger, Maurice, Thérèse, Alida,
François, Maria, Charles, Antoinette, Albertine,
Albert, Julie and Julien.

Contents

Dedication	....	v
Acknowledgement	....	ix
Foreword	....	xi
The Runaway	Antonio	1
The Maggies	Antonio	15
The Wreck of the Alice Mae	Antonio	29
Martin Turbide	Antonio	33
Tales from the Gulf	Antonio	39
Showing the Way	Antonio	49
Guardian Angels on Call	Roméo	55
A New Stage	Roméo	63
Family Tales	Roméo	69
Spanning the Bridge	Roméo	73
Schooldays	Roméo	79
The Bicycle	Roméo	89
General Cambronne	Ludger	101
Man Overboard	Ludger	105
The Dream	Ludger	109
The Main Event	Ludger	113
The Sentence	Roméo	117
College Days	Roméo	125
On Hard Times	Roméo	135
How I Discovered Electricity	Ludger	141
Higher Learning	Roméo	145
A Master Carpenter	Ludger	153
The Lumberjack	Ludger	159
A Secondary Education	Antonio	171

The Universal Joint   Antonio 177
Maurice Gets A Car   Antonio 185
Inspector of Fisheries   Roméo 191
The Salt Fish Board   Roméo 201
War Years   Roméo 207
The Saguenay   Antonio 213
With the Air Force   Antonio 223
L'Évangéline   Roméo 227
Tchaikovsky's Fifth   Antonio 233
L'Île D'Amour   Antonio 237
Safety in the Workplace   Antonio 241
Blessings of the Poor   Ludger 247
The Lure of the Maggies   Donna 251

Acknowledgements

Special thanks to my children Louis, Denis and Colette for their encouragement and support throughout this undertaking.

A special thank you and all my love to my wife Donna who convinced me that these tales were worthy of publication and who guided me along the way. Thanks to Andrea and Hayley, our first listeners and critics for their pertinent comments.

Thanks to Sharon Nicholson for a thorough reading of my first manuscript.

Thank you to Cynthia deKluyver, Editor of The New Brunswick Reader (Telegraph-Journal, Saint John, NB), who first published several of the stories in this collection.

Foreword

What it's about...

It's a kaleidoscope of adventures, romantic episodes and childhood flashbacks. It chronicles the joys and trials on a long winding road towards the unfathomable.

I have lived the life of an unrepentant wannabee. I was a teacher, a soldier, a musician, a journalist, a videographer and an artist; but, mostly, I am a man on a quest for the next bend in the trail.

My brothers Roméo and Ludger have contributed several pages to this book – they are our guides on a tour of the first half of the 20th century.

Roméo explored many careers from fisheries to printing; he taught at Jean-de-Bréboeuf College where Pierre-Elliott Trudeau was one of his students.

Ludger's life as a lumberjack, a monk, a building contractor and now a skilled artisan provides special focus on the rewards of transition and the permanence of change.

Although the stories are presented in a loose chronological order, each is a stand-alone. They are tales and anecdotes offered in a creative non-fiction mode.

Roméo D'Amour

I seldom saw Roméo. Except for the nine months he worked as Fisheries Officer in Baie-Ste-Anne, he was never home as I was growing up. But, whenever we could get together, we enjoyed each other's company. Roméo was a master storyteller who took a life-long interest in the Napoleonic era and whose favourite author was Victor Hugo.

In the late 1970's, I dropped in for a visit at his apartment in Montreal. He was then still rated as one of the best cost evaluators for printing jobs anywhere in the country. It was shortly after supper. After a few minutes of small talk, Roméo placed a bottle of Golden Wedding Canadian whisky on the table and we each took a glass. He pointed to a pocketbook.

"Did you read 'Papillon'?"

"I don't think so."

"It's an amazing story."

We started on the bottle and he began right from page one. He told me the whole story – all from memory – with the details, highlights, special phrases and expressions that had particularly pleased him. That night, I relived those special evenings when, in the old days, he would tell us tales that seemed to come to life on a special stage he could build in our minds.

Soon it was daylight. The bottle was empty. Time for a snooze.

In 1982, he came to my home in Bathurst. As we were savouring a glass of wine, my son Louis came in and joined us. Roméo reached down by his chair to pick up two three-ring binders from a much damaged plastic envelope.

"For the past few months, I've been writing about my childhood and my early years in the workplace. I don't know if it could be of interest to anyone but some of the stories can provide a glimpse of yesterday," he said with a shy smile.

I glanced at the contents. One was entitled "Fond Memories", the other "Douce souvenance". Both were written in pencil.

"I'm sure I'll enjoy reading every one of those stories."

"I believe you will, Antonio; and, since you're in TV production, maybe you'll find some use for this someday. In any case, they're yours and I would appreciate it if you made some copies and passed them around to the family. You're all in there, in my fond memories."

We went to my office where Louis made a few copies while Roméo examined the video production equipment and asked questions about our work. Then he left on his way to Moncton. That night I savoured both books.

In 1986, Emphysema, the official ambassador of the tobacco industry, murdered him. He wasn't quite 72 years old.

Ludger D'Amour

My sister Geneviève has a snapshot of 16-year-old Ludger riding his bicycle; I'm sitting on the bar, 16 months old, and holding on to the handlebars. Shortly after this photo was taken, Ludger went on his quest for life. He was a carpenter helper, a lumberjack and (for seven years) a monk. So, for more than twelve years he was out of my life.

Ludger has an unquenchable thirst for life's educational experiences. He's an accomplished cabinetmaker, a master carpenter and builder, a highly successful businessman in the production of metal shelving units for grocery stores. I marvel at his great talent in woodcarving and celebrate his successes as a luthier. I'm sure he has as many friends in the art world as in the world of business.

Ludger is a genealogist obsessed with the exact fact. He stands out for his incredible memory that can, at a moment's notice, provide a name or describe a scene from decades past. In the year 2000, my wife Donna and I went with him and his wife Henriette to visit the Magdalen Islands. He knows everyone there and he proved to be an inexhaustible source of stories, songs and anecdotes.

In 1985, he published "Épisodes de vie", a wonderful trip down memory lane with stories that span half a century. Last year, Donna and I undertook, with his blessing, to adapt these marvellous tales to English. Check out "How I Discovered Electricity" and "General Cambronne" both are classics. Several of these English versions were published in the Saint John Telegraph-Journal.

He is a close friend. Although he lives in Quebec City and I'm in Cape Breton, we talk almost every day and sometimes several times a day. And, because of his persistent prodding, I undertook this collection of short stories. He was with me every step of the way in the development of the book to provide the first hand observer's point of view or to sketch a unique character.

I hope to enjoy many more productive years with him.

The Runaway
Antonio D'Amour

"When I go out for my daily walk, I often think that before me is the same vista that lured your grand father, Louis D'Amour, to run off and become a sailor," wrote Roger Ganachaud, a friend and distant cousin from Noirmoutier (France), on June 9, 2000. *Those words took me back in time, back to 1874 where I linked up with my ancestor, then a young boy of fourteen.*
He had a tale to tell.

My small island home of Noirmoutier, off the coast of Brittany, is the perfect setting to dream of tall ships and adventures on the high seas. But my father had chosen farming; or, maybe, farming had chosen him. The curse dated back several generations spent in poverty and exhaustion from trying to make a living on our tiny plot of land.

To make matters worse for me, there were too many boats in the harbours of Noirmoutier and too many ships sailing by. This constant maritime traffic beckoned. I envied my friends who often went out to sea with their fathers, either as fishermen or traders, sometimes both.

Last year I went to Lourdes. It was a pilgrimage organized by our parish priest and we joined up with dozens of youth groups from all over Brittany. It was a memorable experience for most of us because we had never before left our communities, especially to travel hundreds of kilometers. For me it was the discovery of an immense unknown world and it came with the realization that it was only a very small part of what was left for me to discover and explore.

Lourdes was a deeply spiritual experience but it also awakened the demons of wanderlust that had forever inhabited my daydreams fed by the dullness of our existence on our small farm and enhanced by a desire to find lands that didn't carry the scars of wars and the ensuing misery.

The people on my small island of Noirmoutier knew a lot about the desolate conditions of our country in this year of our Lord 1874. The heavy maritime traffic in our area carried more than cargo, it brought the latest news from all parts of the world and the saddest news came from Paris. France was poor, exhausted from centuries of wars in futile efforts to satisfy delusions of grandeur. Our present condition was uninspiring and our future appeared rather bleak.

Papa died two years ago. He wasn't sick very long, "just extremely tired," he had said. I was twelve years old, the eldest, with three younger sisters. Julie was ten. The two of us daringly challenged life by quitting school and trying our hand at working "for a living". We worked hard in the field at home; on occasion at the wharf we would sell food and water to the working men. For more than a year, and to our delight, life was sometimes good or at least always bearable because of our efforts.

One afternoon in late August, as we had just finished digging up a long row of potatoes, Roland came over. He was our neighbour's son, one year older than me and already a man.

"Louis, there's a wedding in the village and the feast will begin shortly. Want to come over with me?" he asked.

"I want to go too," said Julie.

"Can you wait for us to get washed up a bit?"

We could hear music and noisy celebrations long before we got to the field where everyone was gathered. Couples were dancing to fiddle and accordion music. Julie wanted to get to the sheltered side of the house where the musicians were. I followed. It was a wise choice as we could see everything. Some of the dancing was synchronized and elegant, a few couples staggered with grotesque moves that owed more to our potent local wine than to the beat of the music. Some of our neighbours surprised us with behaviours that suffered little inhibition. I guess that is how the older generation passes on culture and traditions.

Time passed and Julie dared me to dance with her. To my relief, Roland showed up on cue and off they went. I laughed at Roland's awkward efforts to dance with Julie and wondered how my little sister had ever learned to move so gracefully. The musicians stopped for a generous helping of wine and I went over to the little square. Roland and Julie were standing there, holding hands bashfully.

I was no more than ten paces from them when the most beautiful girl in the whole world stepped right in front of me. She was my age, dark-haired and with eyes that would haunt my dreams for years to come.

"I-I'm sorry," I stammered.

"I'm not," she said with a laugh. Julie joined us and I could feel my face turn red with embarrassment.

"Geneviève, make him dance so he'll stop watching Roland and me," teased Julie. Just then, the music started.

In a flash in my mind, I became a dancer, a poet, and a man of unequalled abilities; however, it did not translate as one of those victories of mind over matter when I tried to speak or move. I still can't understand how she could overlook my mumbles and stumbles, holding on to my hands as we hopped to a country gigue. When the dance ended, she tapped me on the shoulder.

"Bye, Louis," she said. Off she went to join her parents who were leaving the party. I could still show you exactly where her fingertips touched my skin through a tear in the back of my shirt.

I followed Julie and Roland on the long walk home; good thing too; otherwise, I would have wandered all over the island with my head in the clouds and my left hand reaching over my right shoulder every now and then trying to re-capture the thrill of her touch. We stopped in front of Roland's house where they exchanged some words in a low voice and silently we made our way back to the house.

I believe we were both surprised to see the candle still burning. It was long after dark and my mother was usually in bed at that time. Could it be that one of the girls was sick? Quietly we opened the door and surprised my mother in the arms of a man. I was in shock. He grabbed his cap, mumbled a good night and left. Mother stood there defiant.

"Well, I don't believe I need your permission. Gustave is a perfectly good man and he will be moving with us. There!"

"I might have something to say about that... You're wrong, Gustave is not a 'perfectly' good man and he's not moving with us." I replied and I looked at Julie for support.

"It breaks my heart to see the two of you working from dawn to dusk; you're too young to take on such responsibilities. With Gustave, things won't be so difficult and I believe our family needs a father."

"We have a father. He may be dead but he's still our father. Looks like it didn't take you long to forget."

"Please, Louis, don't say anything you will regret later," said Julie.

"Yes. You're right, Julie. Let's all get some sleep and we'll discuss all this tomorrow," begged Mom.

"When is Gustave moving in?" I asked.

"Tomorrow."

"Then it's all decided," I mumbled as I picked a flimsy blanket, removed my old boots and pretended to go to sleep. Mom blew out the candle and the house fell silent.

In spite of my anger, I fell asleep. Geneviève's smile came to me and dissolved into Gustave's grimace that, in turn, faded to be replaced by my Papa's serene face; the kaleidoscope played over and over in a frenzied nightmare. I woke up and looked out the small window. It was still complete darkness.

I slipped on my boots and noiselessly left the house. For several minutes I walked briskly, going toward the sand bar that linked Noirmoutier to the mainland. I guessed that the tide was still going out and hoped that I had time to cover the 4-kilometer run.

I turned to have a last look in the direction of my little home. I spotted a weak orange glow; Mom had re-lit the candle. With tears in my eyes I broke into a run for the mainland.

From the time I was ten years old, I had tried to get my parents' permission to try for cabin boy in the French Navy and had pleaded for their understanding. At first they tolerated my musings, then they became hostile, fearing that I really meant what I was saying; confrontations occasionally turned into rows where I would be cuffed on the side of the head. In spite of it all, or because of it, my determination grew. At first I had planned to hitch a ride on one of the many boats that came to the wharf nearby, but there was always the chance that someone from Noirmoutier would be on board and make my escape more difficult or at least ask embarrassing questions. Then, when my father died, everything was put on hold. But with this newcomer taking over the house, I had to leave and answer the call of the sea.

Diffused sunlight was breaking over the hills when I started north on the road to St. Nazaire. Everyone knew St. Nazaire was developing into a shipbuilding and maritime shipping center and that's where I wanted to be. I walked at a good clip, looking straight ahead, shoulders back like a man who has just shed a heavy burden. There was a persistent happy little tune in my head, a dancing song with which I kept the beat. Like most people in France in 1874, I had no money; and had seldom seen any. I hadn't taken any food for the trip, either; but I was confident that I could go a long way.

The sun was high and the trip taking its toll when I spotted an apple tree near the road. I looked around. No one. I picked three apples from a lower branch and took to the road again. The afternoon sun was torrid and on my left the sea shone with a million tiny silver lights dancing on the waves. My step got heavier, the happy tune of the morning walk muted by fatigue.

Then the sun was a big orange ball sinking slowly into the sea. I had to find shelter for the night. There was a farm downhill from the road, for a moment I wondered if I shouldn't go to the house when I spotted a haystack a short distance away. I lined up my approach in defilade from the house, behind the mound of hay, and walked over cautiously.

"Hurry up! You don't want them to see you, do you?" the haystack said.

I froze. There was a slight movement in the lower part of the stack and a face peered out anxiously through strands of hay.

"Hurry! Hurry!"

I slipped in the hay, feet first, a short distance from the individual.

"Are you alone?" I asked.

"Of course I'm alone!"

"My name is Louis D'Amour," I said formally.

"Léon's my name. Where are you from?"

"Away."

I felt that, if this fellow would not give his full name, he wasn't to be trusted; however, the day had been stressful and tiring; I fell asleep immediately. Before dawn, I was on my way. Léon followed. It had been a warm night but now clouds threatened and soon a quick shower soaked us to the bone. Then a warm August sun quickly dried everything in sight. After a while, we were almost hoping for another cloudburst. In mid-afternoon, we reached the top of a small hill, below to the right, there was a little house snugly set in a cluster of trees. A narrow trail led to the place.

"This is what we'll do," said Léon. "We'll circle to the right and get to the back of the house on the other side of the hedge. We'll pick some grapes, a few things from the garden and, if we're lucky, a chicken..."

"Of course you noticed the big black dog going toward the house."

Léon burst out laughing. "No. I missed that. Maybe..."

"Let me try another way, first," I said. "Wait for me here."

Léon started to say something but I was already on my way.

The dog stood next to the open gate waiting for me to get closer. A low cavernous growl warned me that he was on guard. Two paces from the mastiff, I crouched and the dog came over for the inspection ritual. Partly hidden in the doorway, an elderly woman was watching the scene.

"If Bruno says you're okay, it's okay with me," she said. "What do you want?"

"My friend and I would like to know if you need help with the harvest."

"Are you two willing to work for food and shelter?" said a gruff voice from behind the little shed.

"Food and shelter sound fine to me."

"Get your friend down here. I want to see you both before I decide."

Léon remained seated on the grass until I walked right up to him with the message.

"Work for nothing! I've done enough of that for a lifetime. Count me out."

"Fine. I guess I'll stay there for a few days. I need them as much as they need me, right now... Well, good luck, Léon," and I held out my hand.

"Wait a minute, will you? I'm not sure I like this, or rather I'm sure I don't like this at all... but do I have any choice?"

"Look, if you come with me, I don't want any monkey business."

"Ah! Get off your high horse, I'm sure I can put in as good a day's work as you anytime, my friend."

Édouard was waiting, Bruno at his feet.

"You boys look strong and healthy. That's what I need because there's a lot to do and little time left. But I don't ask a man to work on an empty stomach," he said, and turning towards his wife, "Céline, find something for them."

In an instant there was a feast waiting for us under a big beech tree. There was a generous portion of goat cheese, some bread and some slices of dark meat that we washed down with a few gulps of wine. We ate with appetite, noting that our hosts were watching us with obvious delight.

For two days Léon and I worked hard, making certain that Édouard and Céline would have plenty of supplies securely stored to see them through the quiet season. Then it was time to continue on towards St. Nazaire.

Each of us carried a burlap bag full of food. Céline had given us a few pennies and, as we were walking away, I noticed that she was wiping her eyes. That brought to mind the pains I had certainly caused my Mom and my little sisters. Édouard escorted us back to the upper road. With a heavy heart, I walked in silence.

"You will always find food and shelter *chez Édouard et Céline*, remember that, both of you," he said as he held my hand in his powerful grip.

The rumours were right, St. Nazaire was the place to be. There was traffic everywhere, people, horses, donkeys and wagons; men were moving large stones on the shoreline and lumber was piled high along two big wharves under construction and repairs.

We wandered aimlessly for more than an hour.

"This is a great place to learn a trade," said Léon.

"Seamanship is my trade."

We stopped to admire a beautiful ship at anchor, a short distance from the main wharf. The large building behind us seemed to attract a lot of visitors. We decided to investigate. As we were going up the long flight of stone steps leading to the main entrance, three sailors came out. I noted that their uniforms were clean, their manners happy and self-assured. I could picture myself dressed like that. I watched them walking up the street and I decided to check out that building.

Léon was fascinated as he watched the complex operation of rope and pulley staging techniques that moved enormous loads on the new wharf structure. I started up the steps. He followed, constantly looking over his shoulder. Before I could prevent it, he bumped into a gentleman in a dark uniform decorated with gold braids.

"Better look where you're going, young fellow," said the officer.

"I'm sorry," stammered Léon to the gentleman who ignored the apology and hurried on his way.

"I was just going to ask him for information," I said.

"Why didn't you? You didn't get in his way, I did."

"He didn't look in a very good mood for conversation."

"Look, I said I was sorry."

"Let's go back across the road. Maybe that man over there can tell us what to do to join the Navy."

As we got nearer, we noticed that the middle-aged man sitting in front of a small store was ugly, dirty and under the influence. The little store didn't have that much appeal either so we decided to look to someone else for information; however, the man stood up unsteadily and stopped us as we walked by.

"You look like fine gentlemen and I believe you're strangers. Let me show you around town and later on we'll spend the evening at my place. We'll have a drink and enjoy ourselves. What do you say to that?"

Léon looked at me and we burst out laughing.

"Two good-looking young men," said the drunk as he reached to put his hand on my shoulder.

I brushed his hand aside and, as we continued on our way, we spotted two sailors coming in our direction.

"Don't bump into these guys," I suggested.

"That might not be wise," he said with a grin. They stopped in front of us. "We're looking for a driver with a team of strong horses. Do you know where we could find that not too far from here?" asked one of the sailors.

"We're not from here," I answered. "But I'm afraid there's so much work going on at the wharves that you may have trouble getting what you want."

"I can always requisition the services but I was hoping I wouldn't have to. As you said, everyone is in a hurry around here"

"We want to join the navy," said Léon. "We were told to come to St. Nazaire but where do we go from here?"

"You see that big building over there?" one of the sailors said, "Philippe Verdier (Mister Verdier to you) is standing by the door. Report to him and he'll take it from there."

"Thank you, sir, and good luck with your horses," I said.

"I just spotted them going towards the point. Let's go, this should be fun."

They started down the side road and we headed up the stone steps to report to Mr. Verdier who seemed to be either tired, bored or annoyed.

"What do you want?" he asked.

"We want to join the navy. Is this the right place?" I asked.

"Maybe," answered the sailor. "Go up to the second floor. An officer there will tell you if Captain LaBerrer will see you."

We entered the building and, at the foot of the stairs, stopped to check each other's appearance. There was too much that could be improved on so we limited ourselves to getting our hair in a semblance of order. Then, we went smartly up the long staircase. The entire second floor was like a vast warehouse with barrels, enormous coils of rope, pulleys, and an assortment of tools. Dozens of wooden crates were piled high creating a sort of corridor. At the far end we could see a man at a desk silhouetted against a large window. We took a few steps in that direction and suddenly, a naval officer, coming from behind a stack of rope coils, blocked the way.

"Where do you think you're going?"

"We would like to see Captain LaBerrer," I answered.

"Now, what business would you have with the Captain?"

"We want to join the navy."

"Wait here – and I mean wait here – don't wander about."

The officer went over to the man at the desk. They spoke together in a low voice for a few minutes. Finally, he came back to us.

"You go first and keep in mind you won't get a second chance if he turns you down", the officer said to me.

It was a long unnerving walk between those rows of crates. The Captain didn't look up from the documents he was studying. I stood there immobile and getting more uneasy by the second.

"So, you want to join the French Navy," said the captain without looking up.

"Yes, Captain," I answered.

"What's your name?"

"Louis D'Amour."

"Where are you from?"

"Noirmoutier."

"How old are you, Louis?"

"Fourteen."

Finally, the captain looked up. He handed me a paper covered with words and numbers.

"Here, read this."

I hesitated.

"Can you read?"

"Yes... Yes. But I've never seen anything like this. It looks like an order for supplies with quantities and prices..."

"That's what it is. Now read the underlined part at the top."

I cleared my throat and began, "Official authorization for payment. Must be submitted to the Bordeaux Port Authorities."

"That will do," said the captain and, turning to his left, "Monsieur Dupuis, fill out the papers and we'll take him on a 30-day trial."

Léon's turn took a bit longer because he was nervous. Watching him, I was worried he would pass out before the end of the interview. Finally, another sailor was called to Monsieur Dupuis' desk and told to escort the new recruits to the ship.

Once outside, we couldn't believe our luck. Léon slapped me on the back. "We're sailors, Louis. Can you believe that?"

"No, you're not sailors yet," said the escort. "I think you're about to become cabin boys. In two years from now, if you're still with us, you may be sailors... Right now you're nothing. Understand?"

"Yes, sir!" I answered.

"Don't ever 'Sir' me. When we get to the ship, I'll introduce you to the crew, pay attention to what I say. If I say 'Sir' to someone, keep that in mind because saying 'Sir' to the wrong man is a black mark against you. Remember that."

"Yes, Sir... I mean..." now I really felt foolish.

His frown changed into a bright smile as he offered his hand "My name is Christian-Pierre and I'm very happy to have the two of you with us on Le Zenobi."

We all shook hands with enthusiasm. My whole world was one big smile. Le Zenobi was a very elegant ship, a new brig of white oak. As soon as we got on board we began to strut around like a pair of new owners. Two older sailors came up and solemnly handed each of us a pail and a brush. We were ordered below deck.

Training in the French Navy had begun.

The Maggies

(Les Îles-de-la-Madeleine)

Antonio D'Amour

Le Zenobi **left the islands of Saint-Pierre et Miquelon** very early on Saturday, December 9, 1876. We knew not what to expect from late fall weather in the Gulf of St. Lawrence.

"It's best not to plan ahead. This can be one of the nastiest areas anywhere on the Atlantic," the Captain warned us as we were leaving harbour.

Miquelon Island was just out of view when the first squall hit us. It wasn't full daylight yet and this dark sky merged on a black sea warned of rough hours ahead. This was my second trip to the area in the past two years. It was said by the experienced sailors that every visit to our miniscule North American colony was to be memorable. On my first voyage I had experienced the worst summer storms ever; and, now, howling winds were threatening with mountainous seas sprung on us as if under the spell of a crafty and very malevolent sea demon.

The topsail on the mainmast wouldn't re-position. We scrambled up the ratlines and inched along the footrope to the very tip of the spar. There, 20 meters above deck and over an angry sea as the ship pitched and rolled, Christian-Pierre and I tried to set the rope back on the pulley; after a few misses, the line jumped into place.

"It'll be a long day, *mon ami,*" said Christian-Pierre with a happy expression on his face that told how much he enjoyed these challenges.

On Sunday, I don't remember any daylight except for a few hours of gray gloom. The nor'wester was determined to force us off course. We were hoping for Halifax in a few days and then Boston. February would find us in the Caribbean Seas and I was looking forward to warming up my core in this most hospitable part of the world. But for now, Philippe Verdier was at the helm and he needed assistance.

"We'll be forced to find shelter at *Les Îles-de-la Madeleine* if this keeps up," he yelled as Captain LaBerrer came up on deck.

"We're headed north of Grande-Entrée. Set the course southwest by west for now. I'll be back in a few minutes," said the captain as he disappeared below deck.

It was four o'clock on Monday afternoon when, in near total darkness, we approached the northern tip of Grande-Entrée Island. The area is notorious for sandbars. Captain LaBerrer gave his crew a remarkable demonstration of seamanship as he commanded the maneuver cautiously up a channel not much wider than the ship and dropped anchor in an interior bay. We were sheltered and safe to wait out the storm; finally, we could go below to warm up while enjoying our first hot meal in two days and then settle in for a good night's sleep.

Day broke sunny and viciously cold on Tuesday, December 12; and, to our dismay, the ship was surrounded by a shiny and solid sheet of ice. We set to work breaking the ice away from the hull and added a few wooden planks to cordon off the gap. The extreme cold spell lasted for three days. Thick ice now held the ship prisoner for the season and shattered my dreams of winter in the Caribbean Seas.

A few Madelinots braved the cold for a closer look at Le Zenobi. Some even came on board for a few minutes but we were kept busy getting our ship ready to survive the cruel winter months. At daybreak Thursday morning, a few horses and sleds with about 10 onlookers came to the ship. A Mr. Turbide from Havre-aux-Maisons requested permission to come on board.

"Welcome to *Les Iles-de-la Madeleine, Mon Capitaine*. You may be with us for some time because I believe that winter is here to stay. We've come to offer assistance to you and to the crew of Le Zenobi"

"In the name of the French government, I thank you very much, *Monsieur Turbide* for your kind offer of hospitality."

Captain LaBerrer took him to his quarters where they explored ways and means by which seventeen Frenchmen could temporarily integrate Madelinot society. Shortly after, the two men left the ship to meet with the local Parish priest.

Saturday afternoon, with a generous sprinkling of heavy snow, the ship put on airs of an ice palace. Certain areas were relatively warm but we knew that it would be impossible to provide heat and comfort to the entire crew. The captain informed us that plans had been made to billet most of us in the nearby communities. Sunday morning, parade was called right after breakfast.

"You will be more or less adopted for the winter in good Christian homes where I expect you to behave like honorable Frenchmen. You may be living off the ship, but I must remind you that you remain on duty and under my orders at all times. Now, I want you all to dress up in *l'uniforme de parade* and form up on deck in 30 minutes. We'll be attending Mass at the church in Havre-aux-Maisons."

By the time we got on parade, there were at least a dozen horses and sleds with about 20 on-lookers all around the ship. Mr. Turbide seemed to lead the group and again asked for permission to come aboard.

"Mon Capitaine, we've come to offer to take you and the crew to church for High Mass."

"Mon ami, your kind offer is gratefully accepted as we feel that our first duty is to thank the Providence for having met this challenge without mishap," replied the captain.

It was a lively ride to church with every sled in a friendly competition that sometimes translated to an all out race. The accent was different but the words were French and, by the time we got to destination, everyone was in a happy mood. Dozens of smiling faces greeted us as we climbed the steps and entered the church.

Our uniforms were not designed for the Canadian climate and we had long ago learned the wisdom of adding a few layers of wool underneath. But the church had two fairly large coal burning stoves going like steel furnaces; so, very soon, I began to sweat profusely. I noticed that the entire crew was experiencing the same torment. Maybe our predicament was duly noted because the church ceremony was carried out rather quickly; even the readings were short and the sermon was to the point:

"My dear parishioners, again I ask you to live the Christian faith and provide help to those in need. Let's open our homes to the crew of the French ship Le Zenobi."

At the close of the celebration, we were called to attention and, one by one, these hospitable Madelinots picked a sailor.

"You're coming with me," said Zacharie Boudreau.

Havre-aux-Maisons is a small quiet village. In winter, activity is reduced to a minimum, even on good days. Every storm is seen as another opportunity for the men to gather around the kitchen stove and exchange tall tales while setting up an obstacle course for the women who never seem to stop working.

These homes are comfortable and happy. Food is plentiful and adequate. But it took me some time to get used to the music of their language and I had to adopt new additions to my vocabulary with some words resurrected from the old 17th century French to which were added mispronounced English expressions.

Captain LaBerrer had drawn up a detailed work schedule for the first week. After that, most of the men billeted in the homes were asked to report only for weekly meetings where discussions centered mainly on maintaining a disciplined behavior that would not come in conflict with the lifestyle in the Islands. Few incidents marred the good relationship between the men of Le Zenobi and the Madelinots. On a report of the least misdemeanor, the culprit was arrested and confined to the ship under the watchful eye of the captain.

Léon, the other ship's boy and I were ordered to report to the ship three times a week to continue our studies with Madame LaBerrer. Our course program was centered on reading and writing (French and English), arithmetic and basic seamanship, the latter provided by the Captain himself who, like his wife, did not tolerate any slack.

Except for the rigorous climate, the Maggies sometimes reminded me of Noirmoutier. Madelinots demonstrate a strong attachment to their religious faith and are always happy to give help to someone in need; and they're happier if it provides an opportunity to meddle in other people's affairs – so much like home!

I attended midnight Mass on Christmas Eve with the Boudreau family. It was a moving religious ceremony. However, I felt that much of the pageantry had already been provided by the lines of sleds and sleighs each with a little red lantern and drawn by lively horses to the music of tiny brass harness bells. This image of winter caravans winding their way to church under a clear starlit Canadian sky will forever remain in my mind as the quintessential Nativity scene.

My circle of friends and acquaintances grew daily. I was invited to many homes where merry hospitality was the rule. Often, I had the occasion to spend some time with other members of the crew. Unfortunately, Christian-Pierre was involved in some fracas at the little hotel in Cap-aux-Meules and his billet was cancelled as was much of his freedom for most of the time. I often met Philippe Verdier who already seemed to know by name everyone in the area: man, woman or child; he was a very popular guest at the many gatherings that marked the Christmas season.

Zacharie, my jovial host, often asked me to accompany him to his brother-in-law's place where we played cards and talked away the evening hours. And it was there, *chez Alexandre Thériault* that I met Geneviève.

Instantly, she took the place of my other Geneviève – the Geneviève in Noirmoutier who had inspired so many tender dreams. But I was too eager, too obviously attracted to this beautiful and charming young lady and, *Maman Élizabeth Thériault* sensed danger.

Madame Thériault had an aversion to strangers. The farther they were from their homeland, the more she judged them to be scoundrels. Her daughter was immediately given the sternest of warnings:

"Don't pay any attention to Louis D'Amour. He's not one of us and as soon as spring comes, he'll be out of here. The sooner, the better, I say!"

"Why do you say that? Why do you think I pay special attention to him?"

"I see how you look at him and how he looks at you. I swear that, if Alexandre wasn't here to stop me, I'd tell my brother Zacharie to stay away from here until that Frenchman is gone."

"They only come here to play cards, *Maman*. And Louis tells such wonderful stories. I could listen to him all day."

"As the saying goes: *A beau mentir qui vient de loin* (Lying comes easy to those from afar). I don't trust him. I don't trust any of them around respectable women."

These discussions were reported to me by Zacharie who thought it hilarious that anything might develop between his little niece and me. It caused me a lot of heartache because I wanted to get to know Geneviève and for her to know me; but I didn't want to create any problems to that family or grief to Geneviève.

One morning, I discussed my situation with the Captain and Madame LaBerrer. They both agreed that I should move to another home.

As usual, that evening, I helped Zacharie with the barn chores; I took the opportunity to explain that I felt I was the cause of some disagreement in his sister's home and I thought I should move out of their lives, at least for some time.

"You pay too much attention to woman talk. Wait for a while, Élizabeth is just being unreasonable. She'll get over that."

"Nevertheless, I'm in a very uncomfortable situation. I'm sure you can see that," I said.

"Louis, I know of at least half a dozen houses that would welcome you gladly. You'll make your pick tomorrow... I don't suppose you want to come with me *chez Alexandre* tonight for a good game of cards," he said with a chuckle.

Geneviève's older sister Radégonde had a boyfriend, François Chevarie. He seemed to be well accepted by the girls' mother. He often came to Zacharie's house and we became good friends; so, as often as Radégonde was allowed out of the house with François, Geneviève would tag along and we would see each other. But I had another very serious concern.

Gradually, in spite of myself, I had started to plan on staying in *Les Îles-de-la-Madeleine* and that meant becoming *un déserteur,* a runaway from the French Navy. It also meant giving up on my career plans as a sailor, cutting off all ties with France thus becoming an outcast – all for the love of Geneviève.

In early March, an unusually warm day for the season seemed to announce our imminent departure from the Islands. After muster parade, I left the ship quickly and headed for Havre-aux-Maisons. Philippe Verdier had to run to catch up with me and, as we reached Dune-du-Sud, he asked me to stop.

"What's the problem?" I asked.

"I'm not sure how to begin... Look, I'm going to trust you with a secret; it's like saying I'm trusting you with my life," he said in a low voice.

"You plan to jump ship."

"Is it that obvious? Tell me. If that's the case, I'm going into hiding right now."

"That wouldn't be wise. It's much too early and they would have weeks to look for you. Philippe, if you plan to stay here, I suggest you make your move at the last minute, just as the ship is about to leave."

"So, I guessed right. You're planning to stay here too."

"Let's keep this quiet for now. No one is to know because no one can be trusted. I think I have a plan but it needs a bit of adjustment. Wait a week or two and I'll get back to you. I'm sorry, Philippe, that's all I can say right now."

We walked the rest of the way in silence.

A thin line of pinkish gold morning light marked the horizon as dozens of men and boys hurried over an immense ice field looking for the large gray seals and their little white pups. Further out, a black undulating sea threatened, causing the big ice floes to break up with loud noises, like pistol shots.

Carrying big sticks, large knives and coils of rope, dozens of hunters in loosely formed squads of four men walked quickly, their conversations an indistinct hum broken by the occasional yell of someone slipping and falling in puddles of icy water. These are the Rites of Spring in the Islands, the harvest of the seals, the first income generating work of the year. It also happened to be my first involvement in communal activities with the Madelinots.

I was with François Chevarie and two younger men, Nectaire Thériault and Martin Turbide. The four of us got along well together. I noted that, in spite of the treacherous terrain, they managed to keep their balance; I had to tread more carefully. Shortly the first wave of hunters reached the killing grounds and the harvest was underway. I was a bit disturbed by scenes that brought to mind images of primitive man's murderous fury; but my friends accelerated the pace, spurred on by the fever of the hunt and oblivious to my reaction.

Soon I was in the melee, without a stick but with a coil of rope on my shoulder. My job was to string together François' harvest for the long haul back to shore. That's when I noticed that Martin and Nectaire, like me, carried only ropes.

"Who are you working with?" I asked them.

"We have a system," replied Nectaire with a wide grin. "We follow the hunters on their way back because most of them start off with more than they can pull."

"We pick up what they drop off. Usually, we end up with as many seals as the best of them," added Martin.

Everyone returned satisfied with the hunt. There was no loss of life and there was lots of work for the next few weeks. This annual hunting season provided the Madelinots with some of life's essentials.

Carried on a high tide and pushed by a westerly wind, Le Zenobi left her winter refuge and sailed up the bay to the Grande-Entrée wharf on May 18, 1877. Captain LaBerrer had specific assignments for each sailor. The ship had to be ready for the trip to Halifax.

Late that afternoon, Philippe and I left to go to the general store from where we disappeared, as planned.

At dusk three teams of two sailors went door-to-door in a wide search for Louis D'Amour and Philippe Verdier. We were nowhere to be found.

Next morning, the search was suddenly called off because the weather was particularly auspicious and possibly because the captain feared more desertions. Under full sail, Le Zenobi left the Islands and sailed forever out of my life. I had served the French Merchant Navy for more than two years.

We missed the spectacle as we were hiding in a hole under the warehouse, next to a large kerosene tank. Suddenly, the trap door flew open.

"Le Zenobi is under way and I don't think your good Captain LaBerrer will be back here for quite a while. So, get out of that hole and start earning your living as Canadians, you damn Frenchmen!" said Neil McPhail with a hearty laugh as he reached to pull us up on the warehouse floor. I had done some work for Mr. McPhail and I knew he was to be trusted. He was a native of Pictou, Nova Scotia, and operated a business here in Grande-Entrée. He had a few trading schooners and the boats brought a large inventory of building materials, coal and other supplies from his hometown. I was hoping for work on one of his small schooners.

"Come over to the store for a good cup of tea," he said.

While we were enjoying tea and hot biscuits, Mr. McPhail went behind the counter and returned with an envelope addressed *To Louis & Philippe*.

"This will surely come as a surprise," he said as I opened the envelope.

<u>Notice to two deserters</u>
For two years, we sailed together on Le Zenobi. I judged you both to be excellent sailors with good potential to become officers. I'm very sorry to lose you but Fate has mysterious ways and who knows what the future holds for any of us.

I asked Mr. McPhail to pass on another envelope with part of the money owed you for your services these last four months – I don't want Frenchmen to start life in Canada by begging.

As you are deserters of the French Navy, should we meet again, I shall have to arrest you.

Bonne chance et adieu.
(It wasn't signed.)

"I hope that I'll get the chance to thank him some day," I said, my voice choking with emotion.

"Don't push your luck, young man. There's a new life ahead of you; don't look over your shoulder, look to the future," said Mr. McPhail. "There are plenty of opportunities for good sailors all along the coast."

We thanked Neil McPhail and returned to the wharf where we were able to get on a fishing boat headed for Cap-aux-Meules.

"I guess Geneviève will be surprised to see you," said Philippe.

"She knew every detail of my plan," I answered. "Now, however, I wonder how *Maman Élizabeth* will greet the news of my becoming a Madelinot."

Soon we were out fishing and, after a few months, I got work on one of Neil McPhail's trading schooners. Life got a bit easier in the Maggies and my relationship with *Maman Élizabeth* improved somewhat.

I spent a lot of time at Alex Theriault's where I played cards and exchanged stories with family and friends. Little Marie, Geneviève's sister, always begged for more stories about life in France and my ocean travels (years later, she became a nun with the Congregation Notre-Dame). But, in spite of the fact that they always treated me with affection and respect, it took six years to convince *Maman Élizabeth* that I was a good Christian and an honest man.

In 1885, Geneviève and I got married and we moved to Dune-du-Sud in a bright little home on a few acres of fertile land with a small woodlot – a rare possession in the Islands. Maybe these limited successes generated jealousy because the government authorities were alerted, my French citizenship was causing some concern.

In 1887, I reported to Halifax where I informed the officials that I couldn't become a Canadian citizen because of a clause that committed me to fight against my mother country, should the situation arise. I was told not to worry about it. That same day, I was handed my Canadian citizenship papers and my captain's certificate. Considering the overt hostility towards French-speaking people at the time in Halifax, this turn of event was somewhat bewildering.

The Wreck of the *Alice Mae*
Antonio D'Amour

The Alice Mae was full speed on course in total darkness. She was sailing directly for the Magdalen Islands with men relaying each other at the helm. They took turns to warm up below deck.

It was December 30, 1887, the last days of the shipping season and the Alice Mae had left Halifax with full tonnage. Her deck was loaded with building materials and her holds filled with supplies of all sorts. A cold breeze kept the ship at a fast clip. When they reached the tip of Cape Breton, heavy snow was falling and the wind turned into an angry gale.

Earlier that year, in Grand'Entrée, Neil McPhail had given Louis D'Amour command of a brand new trading schooner, the Alice Mae. Martin Turbide was part of the crew of six that had been sailing the Atlantic seaboard with him for the past seven months.

At 11 o'clock, Captain D'Amour told his men to cut sail and break for lunch. They were nearing the Islands and he suggested they warm up before entering harbor. The men completed the maneuver and, in excellent spirit, went down to the galley. On a cold night like this, it was best to warm up the innards. As they were having tea, they felt something had brushed the keel. In an instant everyone was on deck.

"We touched bottom," someone said.

Captain D'Amour couldn't believe it. It couldn't be. In a few minutes the situation became evident.

Everything on board was thrown overboard. Too late. The men couldn't see through the storm but they knew the sinister silhouette of L'Île d'Entrée was somewhere nearby. Sandy Hook, the murderous sandbar, held the schooner in a deadly grip. Enormous waves lifted the ship and rammed her deeper into the sand.

The Alice Mae was digging her own grave.

It was very difficult to lower the sails as masts and riggings were covered with ice. The men risked being dragged out to sea by enormous waves washing over the deck. They tied each other to the masts. After having checked that each man was securely tied, Louis went down to his cabin.

At 27 years of age, Captain Louis D'Amour's sailing career was over. The elegant new ship was dying from the savage beatings of the sea. His crew might not make it. Water was making its way inside and was up to his knees. He remained below in dark meditation. He believed that it was all over. Nothing could be hoped for from their limited efforts. Only divine intervention could help them make it through alive.

His thoughts turned to dear Geneviève who was waiting for him at Dune-du-Sud. Wives of seamen don't sleep during a storm; they stay awake and pray. The lamp must be burning brightly on the kitchen table while little Antoine (one year old on November 6) was sound asleep in his little bed.

Images of the homeland, that country so far away, came to mind.

"Tell me, Louis," his sister Julie had written from Noirmoutier (France), "What is there on the Magdalen Islands that keeps you away from us?"

Slowly, the water had risen to his waist.

"I couldn't figure out what he was doing below. I thought he was dead," said Martin Turbide.

The Captain collected some essential papers and documents; he slipped them inside an oilskin pouch that he tucked in his greatcoat pocket. When he came up on deck, large icy waves swirled waist high around him. With a length of rope he went about tying himself to the mast next to his men who were already suffering from the bitter cold.

They were suspended between an angry sky and a raging sea. Few words were exchanged. They prayed silently, each in his own way. That night, time allocated slowly each minute of each hour. Finally, first light.

On land, some of the men had spotted the masts and could make out through the storm, human forms covered with ice and battered by the breakers. The waves washed high up on shore. The snowstorm got worse. It was difficult to see anything. As soon as the would-be rescuers got a boat in the water, a first wave would turn it upside down and the next one would throw it back on the beach. They tried to throw lines.

All day they fought the sea.

Hanging from the masts, the men could observe in desolation the triumph of the ocean's furious onslaught. The sails were ripped to shreds. The wind whistling in the rigging added a macabre tune to their torment. They were hungry, their clothes had frozen stiff making any movement impossible.

Night returned bringing despair to the heart of those who had managed to remain conscious. The others did not suffer any more. Slowly, darkness covered them in its freezing shroud. The deck was now under water. Waves spit thick foam adding icy weight to the frozen clothes of the victims. Even the toughest men could no longer feel the bite of the wind or the burn of the salt.

But morning returned and, by then, on the shore, Martial Lapierre and his companions managed to launch some boats to come and collect the bodies. They used axes to cut the ropes. Each victim was encased in a block of ice.

The rescuers carried the bodies into the nearest house where they were stretched out around the stove. One after the other, they began a slow return to life. With infinite precautions, kind hands fed them and helped warm them.

They all survived. It was January 1, 1888.

As for the Alice Mae, the pride of Louis D'Amour and Neil McPhail, she sank slowly under tons of sand. What was left of her masts was chopped down at low tide. And there she remains to this day.

But life continued. Captain Louis D'Amour, Martin Turbide and their companions sailed the Atlantic seaboard for many more years and experienced a string of adventures from the Caribbean to Newfoundland.

In 1923, Louis died from kidney stone complications. He rests in the humble cemetery in Grande-Entrée. In the balmy season, the ocean sends tiny wavelets to caress the beach nearby; and, on the last days of the season, when storms smash angry waves on the red cliffs and on Sandy Hook near l'Île d'Entrée, *le capitaine D'Amour* remains undisturbed.

Martin Turbide

Antonio D'Amour

Martin was a sailor. From the age of twelve, he had worked on trading schooners and smaller fishing boats. He had been, in turn, an able seaman, a mate and a captain.

But we knew him mainly as a marvelous grandfather who told wonderful stories of epic adventures on the high seas, and some of these tales are still with us. He sometimes began a story at the breakfast table and continued for most of the day; as it was very detailed and logically developed, we could leave the narrator to go and feed the chickens or the pigs and return to pick up the thread.

His ancestors were those same Basques who first developed the fishing industry in North America and prospered with the support of the Roman Pope's law to eat fish every Friday.

Two centuries earlier another Martin Turbide had arrived in Louisbourg, Cape Breton, from Bayonne (France). Later on, other generations fled l'Acadie during the Expulsion of the Acadians and sought refuge in Saint-Pierre et Miquelon. Then, they stubbornly returned to a difficult lifestyle in Les Îles-de-la-Madeleine.

Somewhere along the way, the Basque label was shelved for the unique Acadian nationality. In many ways "l'Acadie" had been seen as a new start for French Europeans fleeing endemic poverty and abuse by the parasitic aristocracy; and it may explain why the Acadians kept their distance when dealing with their French cousins from France or their immediate neighbors, the more socially structured Québécois. Acadians weren't the proud and independent race some historians have romantically sketched; they were of a rare breed that tried to mind its own affairs, evidently a deadly sin on planet earth.

Martin Turbide was of above average height for the times, at 5 feet 10 inches. He was husky and very strong. His mother was the legendary Luce (Richard-Turbide) who was considered in her days to be the strongest woman in the Islands. Many elders spoke in awe of seeing Luce and young Martin crossing over several boats while carrying a 500-pound load of cod to the wharf, on a stretcher crate.

As a young sailor, Martin had survived at least two shipwrecks and had traveled everywhere along the Atlantic seaboard and the Caribbean Sea. He was first mate on the Alice Mae when it struck Sandy Hook near Havre-Aubert and, for two days was tied to a mast, battered by a raging sea in a winter storm.

Martin was an incurable romantic. He sang old love songs that told of the hopelessness of a shepherd's love for a princess or of the grief of the clumsy huntress who killed her lover while aiming for a wild duck. These songs we heard from him and no one else but I am convinced, even though he sang on key, that writing poetry and musical creations were never his forte; so, they remain forgotten gems of a gallant past.

He was a respected member of the Havre-aux-Maisons community in the Islands.

He was also a devout Catholic. When my parents married, on November 21, 1911, the wedding feast as per traditions was carried out in Martin's house. At the time, the Bishop did not allow dancing. As the party went on late in the afternoon, a strong wind developed with blowing snow.

"If we found a fiddler, could we dance?" asked one of the boys.

"Find a fiddler and dance away," Martin replied.

The party went on until the late hour of ten o'clock, when everyone went home. But, as the storm continued the next day and as the fiddler was still available, the dance started again and went on merrily until the ten o'clock traditional curfew.

The local parish priest wasn't happy when this trespass was reported by one of the scandalized parishioners. So, he decided to make an example of Martin Turbide. However, he had a few problems to deal with because Martin was a well-liked and respected man, he was a generous contributor to his church and he was known to be a bit strong-willed. So, head bowed and with infinite precautions, as a preface to his sermon, the good priest made his remarks.

"We have church laws and they're clearly spelled out. As your Parish priest, it is my duty to make certain that everyone of you know them and show proper respect. Among these laws, there is one that concerns dancing – I must remind you, once again, that it is strictly forbidden! This morning, I regret to inform you that some of our people consider themselves above the laws of the church and..."

His well-planned and delicately phrased remarks were interrupted by murmurs and muffled laughter in the church. The poor man raised his eyes to look at his flock. To his dismay, he saw that Martin had stood up and was taking bows, clearly showing his conviction that what he had done could not be construed as anything bad.

It may have added a bit of frost on the cordial relations between the two men but soon all was forgiven - never to be forgotten.

At age 50, he decided to move his family to the mainland. He wanted to get his sons away from the murderous sea. Martin's wife, Julie, was another Turbide – from a different branch but possibly with the same stubborn streak – and she set her own non-negotiable conditions. She would not leave the Islands unless and until Graziella, her eldest daughter and her husband (my parents) also came along.

My father had a good job with the coast guard. My parents owned a nice home on a hill with a small woodlot for background. They were happy and had never considered leaving Havre-aux-Maisons. But the conflict raged on at Martin Turbide's and it grew from bad to worse. Alarmists whispered that it would end up in divorce – an unheard of crime at the time.

In the name of peace in the family and with a heavy heart, my parents sold their possessions in Les Îles-de-la-Madeleine and moved to Baie-Ste-Anne NB, on the mainland. They settled in the small community of Eel River Bridge where they raised a family of seventeen children: Cyrille, Geneviève, Roméo, Léola, Ludger, Maurice, Thérèse, Alida, François, Maria, Charles, Antoinette, Albertine, Albert, Antonio, Julie and Julien.

And, for nearly three decades, *Grand-père Martin Turbide*, the mesmerizing teller of tall tales of the sea, was for each of us a wonderful grandfather and a charming influence.

In the evening, unless we played cards, there was a lull in our program of activities – possibly to the relief of our parents. Very often, I would sit near my grandfather. He usually had a younger sibling on his knee and he would begin one of his new and usually unbelievable stories of long ago and far away. For decades he had sailed the seas and his yarns were of the sea. It seemed to us that on every one of his voyages, he had had to face violent storms. Inevitably, he would crash on a coral reef or plow into a sandbar to be left stranded on some enchanted island. His adventures took us to Bimini, Trinidad, Jamaica and Haiti. It was almost instructive, always fascinating.

One evening, he outdid himself.

According to this tale, they had left Havre-aux-Maisons, in the Maggies, early on a cold sunny morning and, for the opening narrative, he took us through a detailed description of the maneuvers they had to go through in response to any and all changes in the weather. The trip south was certainly eventful with hourly changes in the winds causing angry seas. The crew was worried.

This time fate was to strike her dastardly blow at a new location, Tamaro Island, just east of Paradiso.

I could tell Dad was listening even though he pretended to read his paper; Mom had slowed down the rhythm of her knitting. We were all mesmerized.

A hurricane had hit the ship, the sails ripped to shreds, one mast torn right off, the other broken in half with rigging and spars flying pendulum-like, striking at the crew. At the height of the storm, the ship piled on volcanic rocks and broke into splinters.

Once again, he was the lone survivor. He managed to stagger to shore where he collapsed knocked out by the effort. He slept through the rest of the storm and, when the clouds cleared and the sun's warmth nursed him to consciousness, he stayed there on the soft sand thanking God for his mercy.

Slowly, he opened his eyes to a wondrous sight. He was surrounded by twelve of the most beautiful girls he had ever seen. They wore only peek-a-boo grass skirts... and the sweetest of smiles.

Tamaro was a bountiful island with tall palm trees and colorful songbirds but it was very isolated. He was trapped. For more than six months he had to live with these pretty angels. Finally a ship rescued him.

After all that time, Grandmother Julie had decided that her dear Martin was gone never to come back. So, it was with great rejoicing that his sweet wife and all his many friends, the Islanders, celebrated his return from another one of his marvelous adventures.

Grandfather Martin was always up at the crack of dawn and he was early to bed. That evening, after he had left for his room, Dad spoke to us.

"Let's see now... Well, you all know your grandfather was a sailor for many years. He sailed to Quebec City, Halifax and Boston. For several winters, he went to the Caribbean Islands. We know for sure that he was shipwrecked twice, once with my Dad in a winter storm. Some of his stories are true. But, please children, forget this one about Tamaro Island, east of Paradiso."

That story lives on.

Tales from the Gulf

Antonio D'Amour

Several expatriates from the Magdalen Islands chose to settle in Baie-Ste-Anne, NB, in the early part of the 20th century. They missed their islands and, every Sunday afternoon, most of them met to discuss the latest news or rumours from Paradise Lost. On bad weather days, the kids were tolerated in the house while the adults reminisced.

In the kitchen and in the dining room, the women carried on an incessant flow of conversation on topics of family matters while in the living room, where a large map of the Islands indicated every shipwreck in recorded history, the men went back to sea. They were all sailors and fishermen. They loved the sea for her ever-changing beauty; they revered her majesty and respected her power; and they acknowledged gratefully that the ocean provided life's essentials.

Early on, the conversation would drift back and forth from happy memories to darkest tragedies.

The story of the Cape Breton disaster was very detailed as most of the men had gathered the information from the survivors themselves. Isaac Thériault would lead off with the theme and others added variations.

It was the end of November 1875. There were seven trading schooners from the Islands in Halifax Harbour. They were loaded with provisions for the winter and ready to leave for home. The day was splendid; however, for several hours they were becalmed. At dusk, a light sou'wester cooled the night air, a good wind; the small fleet was underway. They were becalmed once again off Sheet Harbor.

The evening of the second day, they passed the Strait of Canso and, with full sail, set course for the Magdalen Islands. The night was beautiful; crews and passengers were dreaming of home. At daybreak, a strong wind picked up but diminished shortly after 10 o'clock. An hour later, they rounded East Point, PEI. It was perfect sailing weather and they began to hope for a crossing in record time.

Some time later, a sudden violent nor'wester slammed the small flotilla. Heavy snowfall cut the visibility to less than 10 yards and the gale took on hurricane force.

On the *Marie-Anne*, Captain François Thériault had taken in the sails, leaving out only two feet on the mizzen. He tied the wheel and set course for the Islands. It was a night of horror and terror on a sea demented with waves that dwarfed the ship. Dawn broke and under a blanket of driving snow, visibility was cut to a few feet. A powerful wind over the dark gray sea plowed deep furrows creating towering cliffs that forced the ship off course.

Early that morning, *L'Espérance* caught up to the *Marie-Anne*. She had the wind at her back, no sails and aiming to make it past Cape North.

"You're headed for the breakers off Cape Breton," yelled Captain Thériault.

She sailed on, unable to alter her course.

A giant wave nearly capsized her, carrying away a seaman. However, she made it around the tip of Cape Breton and was left for several days at the mercy of an angry ocean.

Three ships followed: the *Stella-Maris*, the *Artique* and the *Présidente*. The rocky cliffs near Chéticamp were waiting with a white turbulent zone of angry foaming sea hiding shoals hundreds of feet from the shoreline.

With shredded sails in a dervish dance around broken masts, the 52-ton schooner *L'Espérance* neared Chimney Corner. Three crew were at the bow. Through a brief break in the cloudy mass, they saw the ship rushing towards the breakers. Pushed by the storm, *L'Espérance* picked up speed crossing unscathed the outer perimeter of shoals to come crashing on sentinel rocks a few yards from land. Only three seaman survived; as they were thrown from the bowsprit into the sea, a large wave carried them high on shore where, with added terror, they saw trailer waves trying to claw them back into the cauldron. Two rescuers led them to the safety of a sturdy Cape Breton farmhouse where they were warmed and fed. It would be weeks before they could return to Les Iles-de-la-Madeleine.

The *Stella-Maris* was thrown on shore and jammed upside down between two enormous rocks at Broad Cove. Her crew of seven lay dead on the frozen rocky shore.

Dismasted, the *Présidente*, a 40-ton schooner, was caught on the turbultent breakers and rammed on the rocks at Cape North. Her Captain and crew of five saw themselves hoisted high on the ice-covered granite cliffs tantalizingly close to safety. They were later found with broken limbs and fingers torn off from trying to scale the icy rampart.

The *Artique* under hurricane gales left the steel gray stretch of sea to break into a zone of white foamy furrows whipped to a frenzy by the wind and acres of submerged rocks. A friendly wave picked up the schooner and tossed her on a forgiving section of shoreline. All her crew survived the ordeal and, after major repair, she returned home.

The *Painchaud* and the *Flash* also rounded Cape North and, like the *Marie-Anne*, they were adrift for days on the North Atlantic. Finally, all three made it back to Scatarie Island. Then the three trading schooners limped down to Louisbourg for repairs. From there they alerted Halifax.

That sea disaster had also left the Islanders without much needed winter supplies. So, the steamboat Harlow was dispatched from Halifax to bear the tragic news and deliver supplies to Les Iles-de-la-Madeleine. On December 15, 1875, the *Marie-Anne*, the *Painchaud* and the *Flash* returned home.

Tragedies like this encouraged more emigration from the Magdalen Islands towards mainland Acadian villages like Chéticamp and Baie-Ste-Anne.

During those years the schools on the Maggies offered a full ten-grade education. The children benefited from an excellent education for the times and it served them well. The teachers were admired and respected. In Havre-aux-Maisons, it was Pierre Turbide who taught the higher grades; while, at the elementary level, the teacher was usually referred to as the daughter of the Captain of the Flash - no doubt, it was believed that the legendary status of the *Flash* and her Captain, Isaac Arseneau, sufficed to guarantee the schoolteacher a special place in history.

It was a time of embellished legends. The ill-fated *Marie-Celeste* and the mysterious *Flying Dutchman* dominated sailors' folklore. So, naturally, choice selections of these tales were transferred to describe the fate of the *Flash* in 1881, when the trading schooner vanished without a trace in the Gulf of St. Lawrence. The *Flash* had survived the Cape Breton sea disaster of 1875 when a number of ships and crews from "the Maggies" had perished. For six years thereafter, under the command of Captain Isaac Arseneau, the ship had traveled from Newfoundland to Halifax, with the occasional trip to Quebec City. Isaac was a respected seaman, a God-fearing man and community leader. Nothing in his background or about his experienced crew could help clear up the mystery. The years passed, legends multiplied, the enigma remained.

For many years every time a ship left the Islands for the St. Lawrence River, someone on board would take it upon himself to ask questions or to scan the shoreline for a chance discovery. But the *Flash* did not disclose her secret.

On the Islands, as everywhere else in fishing communities, people patrol their shoreline out of habit and curiosity. Many pieces of debris carried by the sea and left on the shore with the deadwood can reveal information to the experienced eye. For decades, the sea kept silent, not a clue turned up.

One morning the out-going tide left a small ladder on the sands of Pointe-au-Loup, in the Maggies. It was a ship's ladder very similar to those made on the islands. An old carpenter positively identified it as belonging to the Flash. After so many years, the rumor mills were re-activated but nothing further developed.

In Baie-St-Paul, on the north shore of the St. Lawrence, there lived a human derelict, an individual not unlike other drifters that harbours seem to generate occasionally.

His name was Normand. He had a haunted look in his eyes. He spoke little and made no sense. He lived to drink. Well-meaning citizens in the area had tried reasoning with him, to bring him around to a more sensible lifestyle. But Normand seemed determined to destroy himself and he was careful not to involve anyone else; so, eventually, he was left alone.

He lived in a fishing shanty less than 200 yards from the wharf. From his refuge he had easy access to food that the fishermen gave him when they returned from their day's work. When he sobered up for a few days, he would do odd jobs for the villagers – just long enough to collect some money to quench his thirst.

Then, Normand took sick. He refused adamantly to leave his shanty. Two older women went to clean the place up and to make sure the poor man would have something to eat. At night, the men relayed themselves at his bunkside. Soon he was beyond sick. They called in the priest for the Last Rites.

Deprived of a daily dose of alcohol, Normand's mind seemed to get clearer as the unforgiving disease progressed.

"Is there anyone here from the Magdalen Islands," he asked Johnny Simard one morning.

"No, not that I know of," answered Johnny. "They come here every now and then, but there's no one from the Islands here today."

Just then, a young fisherman stopped by.

"How's Normand doing?"

"Good. He's still very weak but his head is okay."

"What do you mean, 'His head is okay'?"

"He spoke to me and made sense."

"What did he say?"

"He asked me if there was anyone here from the Magdalen Islands."

"I just saw *La Béatrice* entering harbour five minutes ago," said the young man. "She's from the Islands."

"Did you hear that Normand? Do you still want to see someone from the Islands?"

"Yes, get someone. Anyone."

Captain Albert was just coming up the wharf when Johnny called him.

"You're from the Islands aren't you?"

"Yes," said Albert. "Why?"

"Someone here wants to talk to you."

Johnny stepped out and Albert went inside the shanty. The place was dark for someone coming in; but, as his eyes adjusted, he spotted a living skeleton on a bunk.

"I'm not a doctor," said Albert.

"Are you from the Islands," asked Normand.

"Yes. How can I help you?"

"I have a confession to make..."

"Look, I'm not a priest." Albert stepped outside. "What's going on here?" he asked Johnny.

"The old man is dying. He wants to talk to someone from the Islands."

Albert returned bunkside.

"It's been nearly 40 years now. I was a young cook on the ship *Le Canayen*. We went to your islands to buy a load of sealskins but we got there too late and there wasn't much choice left. Captain Lemesurier was very disappointed and the whole crew knew they wouldn't get paid unless something else came up."

Normand stopped for a while. Albert waited.

"We left Cap-aux-Meules early the next day but were becalmed near Havre-Aubert. There was another ship nearby so we got together and became friends. There was no wind for the entire day. At sunset, a light breeze set us on our way. During the night, the wind died down again and after some time we noticed that our friends weren't very far ahead of us. Someone suggested we put the dories out and drop in on them."

Normand paused for a long time and Albert became uneasy. Just as he was about to get up and leave, the old man continued.

"The Captain told us to be quiet. He went and got our two guns. We sat down on the deck around him and he laid out a plan to board the other ship and steal the load of sealskins and the money. I was terrified. I told him I couldn't do that. But the crew wanted money. I was shaking so much they decided to leave me on board because I might make too much noise. The two dories left and everything was quiet for a long time.

"Then I heard a gunshot, and another. I could hear people screaming (I still hear the screams all the time). Then everything became quiet and soon after I saw that the ship was burning."

"Why tell me all this?" asked Albert.

"Because you must know. You must tell the others, your friends on the Islands... Now, where was I?"

"The ship was burning..."

"They stayed in the dories nearby to make sure that the fire would completely destroy the ship. The sun started to come up but we were still dead in the water; so, they took their time making sure everything that might float was destroyed.

"They got back on board with the skins and some money, which was shared among the crew. I didn't want any so I guess they had to make sure I wouldn't betray them.

"By that time, the boat had burned to the waterline and was about to sink.

Three men grabbed me and forced me into one of the dories. We returned to the burning ship. The body of Captain Isaac Arseneau was floating face up, tangled in some rigging; he had been knifed a number of times.

"He fought like a lion," one of the men said as they hauled the corpse over the gunwales and asked me to hold his head.

One of them then reached over and cut his throat. Then, he turned and pointed the knife at me.

"Why did you do that?" he asked.

"I didn't do anything," I said.

"Well, we all saw you cut the poor man's throat, didn't we?"

"Yes. Yes. We saw you," said the other two.

Normand appeared too weak to continue but, once more, he resumed the monologue.

"As soon as I got home, I ran away to the woods and stayed there for about three years. One day, I heard that *Le Canayen* had ended up on the rocks off Blanc-Sablon and everyone on board was lost. I came back to Baie-St-Paul but life had lost all meaning for me.

"I wanted to tell the story of the *Flash*... Your people have the right to know... We murdered good people and destroyed a good ship for no reason."

He stopped talking and became very quiet. Albert leaned over and realized the poor man had passed away. Respectfully, he backed out of the shanty.

"How is he?" asked Johnny.

"He's free..." said Albert.

As if becalmed themselves, the men were quiet and still for a moment before the storytelling ended and their thoughts had come ashore.

Showing the Way

Antonio D'Amour

Cyrille learned to walk on the deck of the schooner that was taking him and my parents from Les Îles-de-la Madeleine, QC to Baie-Ste-Anne, NB. Although he was only one year old, he must have suffered with my mother the traumatic effect of leaving a beloved birthplace – empathy was an early and constant feature of Cyrille's generous personality.

It was 1913 and they weren't leaving in search of a brave new world. It was a gallant sacrifice to try to appease a major disagreement between Dad's in-laws, the Turbides.

Grandfather Martin Turbide was determined to move his family to the mainland. As a young boy, he had experienced the back-breaking work of a fisherman's son. As a young man he had enjoyed the adventures of sailing. As an adult, he had survived the terrors of two shipwrecks, one in a winter storm. Now an old salt of nearly 50, he was determined to do his best to protect his sons from the nasty temper of the Gulf and the North Atlantic.

A commendable objective that Grandmother Julie didn't entirely agree with. She stipulated that, unless Mom (her eldest daughter) came along, she was staying in the Maggies. Both were of Basque descent; so, one's irresistible charge could not budge the other's immovable determination. Unless Dad quit his job with the Coast Guard and moved to Baie-Ste-Anne, the Islands were to experience the unthinkable, a divorce.

The schooner sailed up Baie-Ste-Anne one late September day. The tide was too low to get close to the inlet that led to Eel River. They spent their first night on the boat with mixed emotions.

"The mosquitoes were as big as flies and a lot more numerous," recalled my father. "I didn't say very much and I knew your mother shared my feelings of uncertainty and disappointment."

The next morning, they unloaded the animals and the furniture.

"I walked behind my two cows, six sheep and one pig while a horse and wagon led the way with all our belongings. I felt like I was getting a taste of Job's misery and I looked apprehensively to the future."

This was the apparently inhospitable setting into which Cyrille was to start out in life. Soon, he was to meet other challenges as there was no school the year he was scheduled to begin his studies. Determined to see his son acquire a good education in spite of these obstacles, my father enrolled him in an English school about 15 miles from home.

The poor boy couldn't speak English and had to adapt to room and board in a loveless environment; nevertheless, throughout his studies, he earned top grades and people marveled at his intelligence and capacity for adaptation. In a test for survival, he was fittest.

Very early in life, Cyrille was fascinated by the evolution of technology, mainly mechanical creations. He was an omnivorous reader and shared generously his latest discoveries with his siblings who sat in for lectures and demonstrations on machines from catapults to rockets. His younger brothers Roméo, Ludger and Maurice spent many hours on complex projects under his direction. He got them thinking not only about how things work but how they were made and how they could probably be improved upon.

When I was born, he was a 20-year-old college graduate in his first year at the Halifax Catholic Seminary. I was told I was present at his ordination but I don't remember; and for more than a decade, for health reasons, he was absent from my life. My older siblings and my parents spoke of him with great respect. In my mind's eye, he was that mystical figure, a sort of role model of unattainable perfection.

Then, I met Cyrille. My first encounters with him turned out to be a lot of fun and excitement. *Père D'Amour* was taller than I expected, and slim - as he was recuperating from major surgery but his health was steadily improving and his environment was unique.

He lived in a nice apartment on the second floor of the Hotel-Dieu Hospital in Campbellton, NB, where he was Chaplain. He had a comfortable living room with a sofa and two padded chairs, a dining room with a table for four, a sort of library and two bedrooms. There were original oil paintings, delicate sculptures and art reproductions. All the furniture was quality wood varnished over dark stain.

He subscribed to many Canadian, French, American and Quebec publications like Newsweek, Popular Science, Paris-Match, Popular Mechanics, some religious papers and magazines, etc. He had collections of books on philosophy, psychology, religion, history, music, art, plumbing and electricity, bee-keeping, poetry, architecture, photography, sailing and gardening. There were at least three sets of encyclopedias.

He played the flute and the oboe and often joined up with friends to form trios or quartets and play Bach, Beethoven, Brahms and the other gods of the classical music world. He had a well-equipped darkroom where we conducted all sorts of experiments using techniques such as cropping, burning-in and dodging; he showed me how to get dramatic cloud effects with the black and white film of the day, using a red filter on the camera.

His record player played Glenn Miller, the London Philharmonic, Gregor Piatigorsky's cello album, most of the music of the era and the classics. He spoke with enthusiasm of the great orchestra conductors Arthuro Toscanini, Pierre Monteux and Leopold Stokowski.

With his close friend, Dr. Ernest Dumont, chief surgeon at the Hotel-Dieu Hospital, he shared music and discussed books that they were reading. I was happy as the silent element of the trio during these exchanges. At 14, I remember reading "*L'homme cet inconnu*" (Man, the Unknown) by Alexis Carrel so that I could take part in the conversation; reading that book was heavy sledding at first but, after some time, I enjoyed the experience. Later on, during lunch, I made some innocuous remarks about Dr. Carrel and, from their delighted expressions, I knew I had scored some points.

They had a sort of a subscription to an art school in Paris that supplied them with rolls of oil paintings that were then shared with other local art collectors in the area; it helped to pay for their own acquisitions.

Cyrille was a constant source of wonder for the teen-age boy I was at the time. He could speak about so many things and savored each and every opportunity to get others to enjoy cultural experiences. Happily, I tagged along on many short excursions and occasional longer journeys in his marvelous and constant quest for knowledge.

He enjoyed many hobbies but I believe photography was his passion.

"Cyrille can't afford underwear," my mother would say. "But you can be sure he has the latest in camera equipment."

In 1947, I was trying to learn the bass fiddle, an instrument that I had to carry sometimes for considerable distances on foot to join up with other teenagers trying to form a band. The bass was a bit taller and much bigger than even a normal size 14-year-old boy like me. I often complained about this. One evening, Cyrille gave me a demonstration with a microphone, a small amplifier and a 10-inch radio speaker that suggested this was but the beginning of greater things to come.

"Some day," he predicted, "your bass will be only a two-by-four with strings and a microphone."

Twenty years later, I was teaching school in Chicoutimi, QC, the Desbiens Music Store put on display a Framus upright bass that looked like a two-by-four hooked to a 20-inch Fender amplifier, as Cyrille had predicted.

I just couldn't resist.

Guardian Angels On Call

Roméo D'Amour

I was only two years old and thoroughly intrigued by that framed color print on the main wall of
the living room, the one depicting a baby sleeping
peacefully in his crib. By the crib, stood a Madonna-
like lady looking lovingly at the sleeping child. And
this lady had wings!

Patiently, my mother answered my numerous
questions.

"Mom, who's that woman with wings?"

"She's the child's Guardian Angel. Each one of
us has such an angel providing us with constant
protection."

"Do I have a Guardian Angel?"

"Yes. You do have a Guardian Angel."

"I want to see her."

"No. You cannot see an angel but you can sense
her presence… Believe me."

I believed my mother. I was convinced that, asleep
or awake, I had my own angel hovering over me, guard-
ing me and warding off potential dangers. I was determined to see her. Suddenly, I would turn my head

and look back. Without warning, I'd look up. I'd close my eyes pretending to be asleep and, quick as a flash, open them. I'd listen for the beat of her wings. Nothing. I figured she was on the alert and bound to elude me. Sometime in the future, I would try again.

At that time, I could walk, and even run, as well as any boy my age. But I couldn't walk up and down the stairs. My mother would not let me attempt it alone, afraid I might lose my balance and come tumbling down the bare wooden steps. There was no handrail, making it possible to fall off directly to the floor below. So, I was still crawling up on my hands and knees; backing down the same way.

One morning, as I got up, I walked to the edge of the stairway. I was wearing a nightdress that came down to my toes.

"Mommy," I called softly. No answer.

I moved over to my left, put both hands to the wall and came down one step. Twice I repeated the move and that put me on step number three. I decided the time had come to surprise my mother and show off my newly acquired skill. But on step three, next to the wall, I couldn't get a good view of what was going on below. I inched my way to the right and, still in a crouch, moved to the very edge of the step. This last move caused my right foot to come down firmly on the hem of my nightdress.

"Mommy," I called again. Silence.

I waited a few seconds before deciding to continue down along the wall. I tried to straighten up from my crouching position but I was checked halfway in my attempt to stand up as my right foot held down the hem of my dress. This pulled on my neck causing me to lose my balance. I was sent diving off step three towards the floor below.

"Mommy," I screamed, shut my eyes and landed softly in my mother's outstretched arms.

Dozens of kisses and affectionate hugs washed away the panic and terror that had filled my soul. Minutes later, after crying had ceased and peace had returned, my mother spoke to me about the dangers of trying too soon to walk down the stairs.

"You can give thanks to your Guardian Angel," she added.

I tried to figure out what she had just said. I wondered if it could be that, when I came diving down, eyes closed, my Guardian Angel had picked me up in mid-air and placed me in my mother's arms.

It was early summer 1918. I was now fully three years old when, one afternoon, as I was playing outside, I heard yells and screams coming from a distance on the opposite side of the river.

There was a man – I could see him – unmercifully whipping a horse, cursing and swearing, making use of all the profanity in his vocabulary. The words were new to me but the tone of the yelling voice and the violence of the horsewhipping gave me a sensation of fear that was minimized only by the distance between him and me.

My mother came out, quickly ushered me into the house and closed the door.

"There's nothing I can do about that," replied my father when, in the evening, he was told about the incident. "Jack is Jack and nothing will change him. He's working hard clearing the land, pulling up tree stumps and heavy stones. I pity Harry, his poor horse, that has to suffer such abuse."

Jack has never come to our home and I have never had a good look at the man. For some reason, I now wanted to meet him. Up till now I had learned of goodness and love, kindness and affection... and Guardian Angels. Now, I was about to learn of violence and evil, curses and devils.

A few days later, my Dad announced that he was going over to the blacksmith shop to have new hinges made for the barn door. Jack was the blacksmith. I pleaded with my Dad for permission to go with him.

The closer I got to the shop, the scarier it became.

The shingles on the outside walls were black. The windowpanes were black with soot. Black smoke was coming out of a truncated chimney. And there was that peculiar smell of burning coal. I wished I had never come but it was too late. I was almost there and, after all, I had pleaded to come along. As we entered, I asked Dad to hold my hand. I was surprised by my father's serene attitude as we walked into the blacksmith shop. He greeted Jack who answered with some kind of growl. He was busy. He had an iron bar in the fire and was pumping the bellows to activate the flames. He added coal and jet black smoke billowed up towards the chimney. The fire got fiercer and the iron hotter. Jack took the fiery red iron bar to the anvil and hammered the end into a loop; then, he brought it to a large tub and plunged it into the water. There was a sharp sinister hiss of steam.

Jack then relaxed for a moment and, now, properly greeted his visitors. My Dad and Jack seemed to be on very friendly terms.

I took some time to study Jack. He was a fascinating individual. He was dressed in heavy dark work clothes. He wore a black leather apron. His leather cap was black as were his rough hands. At one point, he took a stubby pipe from the windowsill and stuffed it with tobacco. He walked over to the hot coals and, with his bare hands, took one glowing lump and calmly lit his pipe. He threw the lump back into the fire, slapped his thigh twice with his hot fingers, talking all the while as if nothing special was going on. My eyes moved away from Jack to survey the blacksmith shop. On the walls were all types and sizes of iron bars, anchors, dozens of horseshoes, nails, hooks, picks, axes, and a multitude of unidentified metal objects.

Jack caught my attention again as he moved to the far wall to pick up a mean-looking whip.

"I just finished this," he said, displaying it to my Dad and describing it with great enthusiasm, as one would a work of art.

"It's a snake-whip and built to last forever," he said proudly.

It had a short thick handle and a five-foot long leash that tapered off at the tip. With one quick motion of the wrist he sent the whip swooshing through the air and hit a wall stud, his selected target.

"Jack, if I were you, I wouldn't use that on Harry," Dad said.

I loved the animals on our modest farm. We had two cows and a calf, a pig, some hens and a few sheep. But there was a bad-tempered ram that daily went through his training routine which consisted of ramming the barn door with gusto.

For everyone's safety, my mother insisted that the animal be tied. The ram got tangled so many times in the wire fence that, eventually, a post was set in the field and he was securely tied to it with a 30-foot rope.

Whenever I'd come out of the house, the ram would take a flying run at me only to be thrown back when he reached the end of the rope. He had selected me for target practice but I had absolute faith in the capacity of the rope and the anchor post to hold the wild one at bay.

One day, in early December, the ground was covered with four inches of fresh snow and the field, with a gentle incline towards the river, offered a perfect invitation for sledding. Cyrille, my older brother, and I took turns enjoying the rides. This time Cyrille was the passenger and I was pushing the sleigh. Suddenly, I heard the rope snap and the sounds of galloping hoofs. I caught a glimpse of the devil a split second before he hit me.

He hit awfully hard. I went sailing over my brother and landed four feet in front of the sled. I stayed down crying, sensing that getting up would provoke another terrifying attack. The ram had run full circle and was poised to strike again.

Hearing the commotion, my mother sensed a tragedy. She came after the ram, swinging a broomstick with amazing speed and vigour. The animal retreated. She took me in her arms, Cyrille by the hand, and we sought refuge in the house. It took her some minutes to dispel the panic, but slowly peace and serenity returned to my heart.

That experience had a traumatic effect on me. For days I would not venture outside the house. Night after night, in nightmares, I relived the lightning charge of that super ram propelling me into orbit. And I would see my mother coming out, broomstick flailing, charging the ram and flying to my rescue.

My mother, my Guardian Angel.

In mid-April, on a bright sunny afternoon, I was granted permission to visit my great-aunt Émilie who lived 200 yards up the road. That trip was always something of a picnic. There was always a wealth of homemade biscuits, doughnuts and lemonade; in this home of adults, a child was king.

They had a Victrola gramophone with a large assortment of records, especially songs of World War One: *Over There, There's A Long Long Trail, Pack Up Your Troubles, Roses of Picardie, Tipperary, Mademoiselle From Armentières, Le chant de la victoire, Le petit conscrit* and some stirring military band music. I could never tire of that magic of the Victrola. There was also an intriguing 3-D viewer with umpteen color postcards, mostly about battles, exploding shells and soldiers at war.

I had always gone there with Cyrille; but, this time, I was to make the trip solo. The snow was almost all gone but the fields were still wet, the roads muddy and the ditches brimful with dirty water. I was proudly wearing a new pair of rubber boots. My mother walked me to the road, opened the gate and kissed me goodbye.

"Walk on the side of the road. Avoid the ditch. Stay away from mud patches and puddles. And walk, don't run."

As I started out, I glanced at the ram. He had spotted me and was trying to break loose. The rope held firm. I turned my attention to the road and avoided the patches and the puddles. I walked cautiously along the side of the road near the ditch where the dirt was drier.

I wasn't halfway to my aunt's place when I froze in my tracks. The ram was heading for the road at breakneck speed, a long rope trailing. He barreled through the wire fence, hopped over the ditch, bounced on the road and came to a standstill about 15 feet from me. I couldn't escape.

I turned around and, blinded with tears, started to run towards the house. I could hear the galloping devil coming after me. I was hit from behind and sent catapulting face down into the water-filled ditch. I choked and gasped as I struggled to regain my balance. I was standing in water up to my chest and did not dare move. Through my tears, I could see the brute waiting for me to emerge; so, I cried to my Guardian Angel for help.

"Hold it, you sonovabitch!" barked Jack the blacksmith.

I turned and saw Harry the horse standing still. Jack was jumping out of the wagon. His snake-whip went to work striking viciously at the ram's face. Terrified by the onslaught, the animal barreled again through the wire fence and took refuge in the far end of the field.

Jack now turned his attention to me, still in the ditch and still crying. Gently, he pulled me out of the water and on the road. He emptied my rubber boots and put them back on me. He wiped my tears with a big red handkerchief all the while re-assuring me that he would personally escort me home. Then he took my hand and led me to my mother who had reached the gate on the run.

"The boy's all right," said Jack, "but tell your husband to kill that bastard ram before he kills the kid!"

My mother thanked him profusely.

I watched Jack, now my friend, disappear up the road with Harry at top speed. Then it struck me: "How come Jack appeared at the height of my despair, immediately after I cried to my Guardian Angel for help?"

Dad heeded Jack's advice and had the ram slaughtered. At my request, he saved the horns. Years later they were still there, in the barn, on the center wall where I could admire them with awe, still remembering the terror-filled instants of two memorable charges.

And I remembered Jack, my Guardian Angel.

A New Stage

Roméo D'Amour

One late December evening, Dad came home with a brand new sled for my brother and me. He brought the sled directly into the kitchen. On the sled, was a box containing a treasure – a new Victrola gramophone with 24 records! As a bonus pleasure, a second box yielded a 3-D viewer and a large collection of colored picture cards. These two prized possessions were to charm my days for years to come.

Every two months, the record salesman would make his round and stop at the store. My Dad would hand him back 12 or so records and take in the same number of new ones.

By the time I was 10 years of age, I had heard just about every song recorded at the time: World War One songs and marches, popular songs, cowboy songs, songs of the American Revolution and the American Civil War, Negro Spirituals and numerous French songs. I got to know them all. All the time, I would hum a tune or sing a song while, in my mind, visiting those far away places seen on the magic viewer.

The Sunday afternoon visit of my maternal grand-parents, uncles and aunts was always a special event; often other relatives and friends came to join them. They had left *Les Îles-de-la-Madeleine*, 100 miles due east in the Gulf of St. Lawrence, to settle in Baie-Ste-Anne. Now, in 1920, more than seven years after their arrival, they were still homesick. These family reunions, although mostly joyful, never failed at some time or other, when reminiscing, to bring women to cry and men to choke with emotion.

My paternal grandfather was still in the Islands, owner and captain of a trading schooner, *La Béatrice*. All the men in the group had been sailors, some for many years. All loved the beauty, magic and majesty of the sea, a good provider for both sailors and fishermen.

My father had a large map of the Magdalen Islands on which the shoreline was dotted with the names of wrecked ships. The men talked about the 1856 maritime disaster when 18 fishing schooners from the Islands were swept ashore on the coast of Labrador – nine of them completely demolished. They spoke in awe of the vicious storm of August 23, 1873 that caught 84 fishing boats, mostly foreigners, anchored near the Islands and drove more than 20 of them to shore.

There was the spectacular Cape Breton disaster of November, 1875. Eight island schooners, all manned by experienced crews en route from Halifax loaded with winter provisions, had run into a violent storm as they passed East Point, PEI. Five ships were wrecked on the north shore of Cape Breton where most of the crews died. Three schooners survived that disaster. One of these was the *Flash* that was to vanish five years later while en route for Quebec City. At the time that mystery was often compared to the fate of the *Marie-Celeste*.

Those yarns of the sea were most fascinating to me and fired my imagination to the point of repeatedly dreaming of howling winds, demented seas, foundering ships, and drowning sailors.

In the summer of 1921, my father, who had been a storekeeper at the Eel River Bridge general store for some years, was appointed manager. He announced that the whole family was moving one mile downstream to the store complex.

I recall walking by the fully loaded horse-drawn wagon on our way to the bridge with our belongings. I had mixed feelings about the change. Leaving my old home saddened me; there were so many fond memories of so many happy days. Somehow, I realized the first chapter of my life was coming to an end. It was a mid-summer day, sunny and bright. I was walking close to the wagon enjoying the sound made by a short stick that I held to the rear wheel for a staccato beat as it bounced from the revolving wooden spokes.

I guess I was daydreaming and, suddenly, there it was, in full view. What a sight! The business center was big and unbelievably beautiful. It was the leap from rags to riches. Thoughts of the old home disappeared from my mind and the future looked so promising. It was the beginning of a new life, in a new and fascinating world that called for exploration.

This was a major business center with a large 2-storey general store, two warehouses, a spacious barn, a pigsty, a chicken house, an ice shed and for us a large 2-storey dwelling. The buildings, located at the south end of the bridge, were so close to the river that a massive eight-foot breakwater had been constructed to try to prevent further erosion by the tides.

First I checked out my new home. The kitchen was like an addition to the main house. It was very large and brightly lit. Upstairs, above the kitchen, was a large dormitory for the boys. Downstairs, in the main house, more than half the area was taken up by a dining and family room; the other half made up the living room and a guest bedroom. Upstairs, four bedrooms. As the men moved in the furniture, I was on the lookout for two precious items: the Victrola and the 3-D viewer.

I rushed over to the store where a wide drive-in area was covered with clean light grey crushed gravel. There was a long sturdy hitching pole. To the left, close to the road, was a hand-operated gasoline pump. Three steps led up to the entrance platform at the center of the front of the store. To the right and left were very large plate glass windows allowing full view of the driveway from any point inside the store.

There were counters to the right and counters to the left and at the back. The shelves were loaded with a large assortment of merchandise. There was patent medicine, cosmetics, groceries, dry goods, hardware, boots, shoes, rubber boots, shotgun shells, gunpowder, barrels of molasses, and a kerosene hand pump connected to a 250-gallon tank hidden in the cellar.

Spare shelving units and counters were upstairs, as the area was used mostly for storage. Here I discovered all the toys left over from the previous Christmas!

"Roméo, come on down. No kids allowed up there except by special permission," Dad said.

I wanted to go to the warehouses but I knew I'd have to wait for a customer to request something that was stored there. It soon happened. This fellow wanted pickled beef.

I followed Dad to the main warehouse. I saw rows of bags of flour piled high with equally impressive piles of bags of animal feed, barley and oats. There were barrels of salt fish, salt pork and pickled beef.

Dad used a meat hook to fish for meat in the brine; he used a saw, an axe and a knife to cut a rather large chunk of meat.

I counted rows of cases of canned goods; boxes of cigarettes, pipe and chewing tobacco. On a shelf were hip boots and common rubber boots. A section of the wall was covered with storage containers for fishing gear, bucksaws, axes, axe handles, pivies, crowbars, wrenches and other hardware items. In the corner were the coils of rope and bundles of twine.

The smaller warehouse held drums of gasoline (for cars and fishing boats, I was told), kerosene, motor oil, linseed oil and turpentine.

The barn could accommodate two horses, three cows and two calves in the north section. The center section had two wide doors through which one could drive a horse with a loaded hay wagon. The south section was used as a garage for the wagons in winter and for the sleds in summer. Towards the back, a long work counter with a large assortment of tools served as the wood-working shop.

The ice-house had its walls and ceiling insulated with four inches of sawdust and, in mid-summer, still held some five feet of solid ice blanketed with a thick layer of sawdust.

Along the shore, the bracework was made up of large logs that were notched and securely bolted together. The cradle was filled with large stones. It formed an efficient breakwater. From the shore, I could scale this eight-foot fortress wall as easily as a ladder.

Such was the stage on which I would play for the next seven years.

Family Tales
Roméo D'Amour

Alida, my baby sister, died in early October, 1922. It happened when I was still discovering the secrets of the store complex. Mother, gravely ill, was hospitalized in Saint John, 150 miles away from us. The whole family was upset and Dad had to find someone to take care of the five children.

Annie was fifty years old, a widow with a grim face and a lousy disposition. She was constantly muttering and grumbling about our behaviour. We were accused of all sorts of misdemeanors and she never missed an opportunity to let us know that we were hard to take. She could sit in the rocking chair for a full evening, barking orders like an army sergeant. She seemed to enjoy picking on me.

"Bring me a glass of water."

"Put some wood in the stove."

"… No, not that way, this way."

Our real mother never behaved like that. We feared to be stuck with her because it didn't seem possible to change Dad's mind and fire her. From every angle, it looked like mission impossible but we got together and decided to work on it anyway. We felt that, if we were to have a temporary mother, we wanted a young woman – and why not? I was always on the lookout for an opportunity to force an end to the misery. Then something came up.

It was milking time. Annie called me to the barn. She always complained about having to do this work. That day, as always, there were flies about and the cows did what came naturally, swatting them with their long lashing tails.

Annie gave me an unheard of assignment: hold the cow's tail while she was milking. First, I held Brindle's tail. My brother Ludger was out there laughing his head off and I knew that he was thinking I looked like a dummy holding on to a cow's tail.

Then we moved on to Bess, the Holstein, a big cow and our best milker. I firmly grabbed the tail and held on while she tried to find relief from the flies. Then, temptation set in. On cue, the cow made a mighty effort to use her swatter and I let go. It had the resonance of a thunderclap. Bess had scored a direct hit, full face!

Annie bounced up and pounced on me, trying to slap my face. I covered up and made good my escape. I went directly to the store.

"Dad, I have to speak to you. It's urgent."

We went to his office where I told him the full story, a complete confession that had both of us laughing like fools.

"I'm afraid Annie is out to get me. And she'll try to get you to punish me."

He came to the house with me. Annie greeted us with a torrent of criticism and accusations leveled at each and every one of us. Then she played the trump card, singled me out as a scoundrel and told Dad what he already knew about the swatter.

"Antoine, I can't take anymore! I want to go home."

"Well, Annie, if that's your wish, pack up your things and I'll drive you home as soon as you're ready."

There was a fair amount of traffic around our place, mostly store customers and salesmen. Every now and then, some unexpected visitor would appear and break the routine. One day, Shabinsky did just that.

He was a Jew. The first one we had ever seen. Oh, we knew something about them. We knew of Judas. There were also the ones who had chanted to Pilate, "Crucify him!" And, of course, Jesus was a Jew – but this had been conveniently forgotten.

Privately, Dad gave us a short briefing on Mike Shabinsky.

"Mr. Shabinsky is a Jew. And a good man. I want everyone here to treat him with respect. Don't forget that he's a friend of mine."

Mike was short, red-headed, always grinning sadly and blinking all the time. He spoke with a strange accent. He drove a tired horse that pulled a shabby sled. His business was buying hides and pelts. The wet, salted, stinking cowhides were right-angle folded over and over to make them more compact and they were stacked at the back of the sled. The pelts were kept in the front and were neat and clean.

Sitting on barrels in the barn, we discussed the newcomer.

"I wonder if he comes from Jerusalem."

"Would he be a descendant of Judas?"

"It could be that one of his ancestors was a friend of Mary Magdalene and Jesus."

"Yeah. That would be something."

The 'I wonder...' and 'Maybe...' helped us review our notions of the Gospel and provided Mike

Shabinsky with the required aura of mystery.

All that day Mike had collected hides and pelts. He came back to the store around seven. It was dark and a powerful snowstorm was building up.

"What are your plans, Mike," asked my father.

"I guess I'll go to Loggieville," he answered.

"Not tonight. In this weather, you'll perish. Unhitch your horse, we'll put him in the barn and feed him."

"Can I sleep in the barn, too?"

"No way. You're coming to the house."

Reluctantly, he followed my father and came into the house. In spite of Mike's objections, Mom prepared a hot tasty supper. Mike took his place at the table but kept his chair a good distance away making sure the sleeves of his jacket would not touch the table. He was very uncomfortable. After supper he relaxed a bit as they discussed business, friends and mutual acquaintances. Mike carried on a pleasant conversation.

Later on, Dad took him to the spare bedroom, the one reserved for special guests; Mike took one look and backed out.

"Antoine, I know I'm very dirty. I stink. Please let me sleep in the barn, that room is too much for me."

"Mike, listen. This is our guestroom. You're my guest and that's where you'll stay. Goodnight."

Next morning, after a hearty breakfast, Mike offered to pay for the room and the meals.

"No. I don't run a boarding house," said my father. "It truly was my pleasure to keep you out of that storm last night."

After many heartfelt thanks, Mike left to harness his horse. Dad went to the guestroom and returned with a look of bewilderment.

"Everything is the way it was last night. The poor man must have slept on the floor," said Dad.

Spanning the Bridge
Roméo D'Amour

Soon after my grandmother died, my grand-father Martin Turbide came to live with us. Mother was his eldest daughter. He wasn't very active anymore because he was getting old and suffered from asthma, but he was a lot of fun.

My father had returned old Mack and he was wait-ing for a good replacement; so, for some weeks, we were without a horse.

One morning, my grandfather asked me to go to his son Alphonse's place and get his own horse, also named Harry (like Jack's) and bring him back home. Harry was a big gray horse and he was mean. Un-cle Alphonse was out fishing and Aunt Gertrude warned me.

"Don't go into Harry's stall, Roméo. He'll kill you. Go over to Will Savoie's place and get Fred to come over and harness him."

Nevertheless, I went over to the barn swearing that no stupid horse could scare me. Then I met Harry. So, as suggested, I went over to get help from Fred Savoie who obligingly harnessed the horse and hitched him to the sled. Once in the driver's seat, I took out the whip and showed Harry who was the boss.

It was a lively ride even if Harry had none of the attributes of a racehorse. When I got home, Grandfather came out.

"Satan would be a better name than Harry for your horse," I told him.

He led the horse to the barn and proceeded to unhitch him. As he passed in front of Harry, the animal tried to bite his arm off but just managed to grab the sleeve of the windbreaker. Unperturbed, the old man took off one of his woolen mitts and slapped him in the face.

"Don't you dare try biting your master," he said.

From the horse's attitude, I guessed that the tone and timbre of Martin Turbide's voice had a much stronger effect that my histrionics with the whip.

Nectaire was a former sailor, and Aunt Émilie's husband. He was a no-nonsense man, tall, straight, severe – the stamp of authority. He was an inventor and had patented many ingenious gadgets, many clever contraptions, all of which were laborsaving devices. He lived upriver near our old home.

Hippolyte, aka "Polyte", was his brother. He lived across the bridge from the store. They were my father's uncles, his mother's brothers. Polyte had also been a sailor; he was more the intellectual type. During World War One, he was a very outspoken armchair general who, with Dad, fought every battle of the war near the potbelly stove in the store. Every evening, they straightened out the battle lines and corrected tactical errors. They knew they were competent coaches for the French Marshals Pétain, Joffre and Foch.

Polyte was also the unofficial opposition for the Federal, Provincial and Municipal governments of the day. These administrations were subjected to constant close scrutiny, criticism or reluctant infrequent approval, based on the latest news. The local Post Office was in his home and he never failed to be present when the mail came in. One day, the mail delivery service came in earlier than usual and Polyte was plowing his fields. He dropped the reins and hurried home to read the papers, forgetting his horse and plow in the field.

Occasionally, Mom and Dad would cross over the bridge to spend an evening at Polyte's place. For the two men, it was like a meeting of conspirators.

It was just past ten o'clock one Sunday evening and I was still up, in spite of the early-to-bed rule, when my parents returned from such a visit. I was caught downstairs and started tiptoeing towards the stairway for a fast exit; I didn't quite make it before my parents came in. Just as Dad was taking off his jacket, the door flew open and someone shouted:

"Antoine, someone broke into the large warehouse, the back door!"

"Please be careful," pleaded my mother as he left on the run.

It was very dark outside. Dad went towards the warehouse, paused and heard footsteps of someone running towards the bridge. He gave chase.

Running at top speed, he caught up with the individual on the second span of the bridge; since Dad was the faster runner, he didn't try to grab the fugitive, instead he pushed him forward causing the poor fellow to fall face down on the rough timbers of the span.

We knew Ernie very well. He was 19 years old and somewhat undecided as to what to do with his life, I guess.

With Ernie by the collar, Dad walked him in the kitchen and sat him on a chair. The poor lad had a very muddy, bloody face.

"Mother, get some water boiling," said Dad.

I sat in the stairway and watched as Dad proceeded with the first aid kit. After some cleaning, the face looked a lot better even though the nose was bleeding and there were several abrasions on the forehead, the hands and the arms. After cleanup, Dad combed the young man's hair.

"Ernie, you never looked so neat," he said jokingly.

"Antoine, what are you going to do to me?"

"First, tell me why you did this. You know that breaking and entering is a serious offense, you could land in jail."

"Don't call the police. I don't want to go to jail. Never again will I do this, never, ever!"

"I don't know what I'm going to do about this, Ernie. First, I'll assess the damage."

"I didn't do much damage, Antoine. Please, give me a break."

"Rest here for a few minutes, to get your wind back. Then, you're going straight home. I'll see you in my office at nine o'clock sharp tomorrow morning."

Ernie showed up on time the next morning with contrition written all over his face. And, as Justice of the Peace, my father always acted his natural self. A strict disciplinarian, he favored quick punishment but he shied away from revenge. He naturally sought to temper justice with mercy.

"Well, Ernie, the first part of your sentence was meted out last night when I pitched you headfirst into the span. For the next part, you can choose between going to court or accepting a sentence from me."

"Please, Antoine, be the judge."

"Ernest, for the next five days, you will report to me at seven o'clock every morning. You will work under my orders all day, without pay. Each day, I'll provide you three meals and one pack of cigarette tobacco... and I'll forget about last night."

Ernie thanked Dad with tears in his eyes.

Schooldays
Roméo D'Amour

Walking two miles to school, sometimes in
heavy rain and sub-zero temperature, wasn't easy on
us. Mindful of this, my Dad oftentimes hitched the
horse and drove us to school picking up other children along the way. Some other neighbours joined my
father on this pick-up and delivery service whenever
stormy weather threatened. On good days, we walked
or jogged the full distance.

I was nine years old in 1924 when my two cousins,
Edgar and Aurèle Thériault, and my brother Ludger
joined up with me on a project to use Uncle Abdon's
rowboat to sail upriver not far from school. Whenever
there was a favorable wind, three of us would stand
up in the little dory, jackets firmly held open to the
breeze; it made rowing easier for Edgar or me. One
day, the tide was up and there was a good fresh westerly breeze, we were taken from Jack's bridge to home
in good time and we didn't have to row, our little jackets did it all.

One morning, at high tide, we drove the boat
ashore and tied it securely. At four o'clock we raced

from school to our dory. The tide had gone down and left our boat almost 10 yards from the water's edge. Quickly, the rope was untied, coiled and tucked in the bow. With great difficulty we spun it around and tried to slide it afloat. It wouldn't budge.

Ludger suggested that we use the oars as rollers. Ahead of the boat we positioned flat stones that we dipped in water to make them more slippery. We got set for the launch, Ludger and me at the bow and Aurèle and Edgar at the stern. I was starboard side.

Everyone gave it his all and the rowboat began to slide quite fast. The bow swung suddenly pinning my feet under the flat bottom boat. I cried out; but, in the excitement of the moment, nobody heard me. Seconds later, the boat was afloat and I was squirming in agony on the slimy stones.

Edgar wanted to remove my canvas shoes but I objected because the pain was already unbearable. In tears, I was carried to the boat. I asked the boys to row at a moderate speed, I was hoping for time to recuperate. When we landed, they carried me up the slope and across the road, headed for home.

From the store, Dad spotted the scene and came out running. He took me in his arms and asked the other kids to follow him. Once in the house, he sat me on a chair and, while they gave a detailed report, he took off my shoes and stockings. Both feet were red, purple and blue; dozens of veins had burst. Mom prepared a tub of water to soak my feet as Dad hurried to the store for bandages. I pleaded with him not to bandage my feet because I felt all the bones had been put out of joint. Thankfully, he reconsidered.

He went to the woodworking shop where he shaped two blocks to fit under my feet. He set them in place and then I was bandaged from toe to ankle. Healing was a slow process that lasted several months.

My feet healed in time for me to get into trouble again. It was the noon recess and the teacher was outside with us. I was on the run to avoid getting tagged; so, I ran into the school and hopped on top of a desk. Perched high, I dodged my pursuers quickly jumping from one desk to another. At one point, sensing the danger of getting caught, I leaped from one row of desks to the next. I slipped and fell heavily to the floor, striking my head on the edge of a desk on my way down. I got up quickly, a bit dazed but glad to be unhurt. My pursuers took one look at me and ran out; then, half a dozen boys came running in.

"Look at that cut! Get the teacher."

They were staring at my right eye and, instinctively, I brought up my hand just as the blood started to flow. The teacher came in, had me sit down and called for all the available handkerchiefs and some water. Now the wound was really bleeding. My face was bloody and my shirt getting more red by the second.

The look of horror I saw on my friends' faces made me nervous; I began to cry. The teacher managed to apply some sort of bandage and then she sent me home with my friends Eugène McIntyre and Edgar Thériault to accompany me.

A short way down the road, I began to feel very weak. The blood had soaked through the bandage and was running freely down my face. My friends helped as well as they could, almost carrying me at times.

Then we got near Jack's blacksmith shop. Jack was plowing his field. He spotted us, hopped over the fence and came running.

"What happened?"

"He's Antoine's son and he's got a nasty gash above his right eye."

Jack took a closer look.

"Mother of Jesus!" he exclaimed. "Sit down here, by the ditch. I'll hitch Harry and drive you home."

He moved fast and in little time Harry came running out of the gate.

I sat on the seat near Jack who was holding me up with his right arm. His left held the reins and the whip... the snakewhip. He put Harry at kickdown speed and in minutes we came skidding to a stop in front of the store. My Dad rushed out to meet us.

"Oh, no. Not you, again!"

I could not say anything. He took me gently in his arms and hurried to the house. Mother almost fainted when she saw my condition. But she found bandages and managed to get some water boiling while Dad removed the blood soaked rag that made me look like a walking wounded of World War One.

He let the blood flow for some seconds, disinfected the wound, closed the cut with his fingers and taped it shut. Meanwhile, Mom had cut up a white pillowcase into wide strips that were used for a new dressing. When my sister Geneviève arrived from school, she gave the family a detailed account of the incident and I received a sizzling sermon. Next morning, head bandaged and feeling okay, I returned to school.

At school we played rough and cruel games. One day, we spotted a flying squirrel up a tree near the school. We converged on the poor fellow and shook him loose from tree to tree until, terrified and completely exhausted, he fell to the ground. We used him as a ball.

We formed two teams: eight boys on one side of the school and eight on the other side. One player from our team threw the animal over the roof to the other group. One boy caught it and came running after us around the east corner. We all ran to the right, the enemy in hot pursuit. If the runner could hit one of us with the squirrel, the prize remained with them; if he failed, our group took over.

We played for about 20 minutes and realized the squirrel was dead.

We had our own brand of baseball with our own handmade ball. No one could afford mitts or gloves so we played barehands. To make the ball we started with a round stone about one inch in diameter; then, yarn from discarded old socks was wound tightly around the stone. Two leather eight-shaped covers from an old pair of boots were soaked in water for the stretch and neatly sewn on with shoemaker twine.

The rules for baseball were fairly simple and non-democratic. Regardless of the number, the players were divided into two groups. Each group then chose a captain who designated a catcher and dispersed the rest of his men to shortstop and field positions. You could have any number of outfielders. Usually, the captain was self-proclaimed and he was the pitcher. The first turn at bat was decided the traditional way with hand over hand on the bat (a very sturdy stick).

The pitcher would throw the ball over the plate, as in a regular ball game; three strikes meant "out", four balls got you to first base. Three men out – we preferred "dead"– and the groups changed position. There were no reasons to have basemen. To put a player out – to "kill" him – the pitcher (only the pitcher) had to hit him with the ball as he moved between the bases. When a runner was hit he was declared dead. During play, anyone getting hold of the ball, had to fire it to the captain-pitcher whose task it was to kill the runner.

Oftentimes I was the pitcher and dropped many a runner.

One day, I was on the run from first to second base; Eugène McIntyre was the pitcher. He was a southpaw who fired a very fast ball. He caught me on the side of the head; I dropped, knocked out.

"You're dead," he called.

Someone threw some water in my face to bring me back to my senses.

Winter called for new games. One day I led my group to prepare for a war game; Eugène, 10 yards away, was getting his own army together. The snow was heavy and wet. First we built the trenches and the parapet; then, we stocked up on ammunition – a dozen snowballs per soldier. We left everything ready for the next day's battle.

It got real cold during the night and the ramparts changed to solid ice. The ammunition was hard and shiny. We scheduled a first battle for the noon recess; our lunch delayed us about 10 minutes and then, the call to arms!

My younger brother, Ludger, was in the other camp. That worried me. I asked Eugène to exchange my brother for one of my soldiers. He agreed, Ludger declined. I tried scaring him by saying that there was no way he could escape defeat with that gang. Safety was at my side. He wasn't impressed.

I returned to my command post and issued the orders:

- Fire only when you see an enemy soldier,
- Remain behind the parapet until you have fired eight rounds,
- Hold on to four rounds for the final assault that will come at my signal.

The battle was going furiously with a rush of missiles from the trenches. We were losing some men but Eugène was paying a heavy price. I sensed a sort of lull in the fighting, ammunition was running low and I guessed the enemy was recuperating our spent snowballs.

So, I led the charge. With a terrifying scream, we leaped out of the trench and rushed across no-man's-land taking some punishment. We cleared their fortifications, straight into their stronghold. The enemy was panicking, some on the run. Braver men met us head-on; we were firing at point blank range and both sides suffered a lot of casualties.

In less than a minute, it was all over. Both armies were out of ammo and out of breath. Neither Eugène nor I dared to claim victory. Our armies had been tested and found worthy.

That's when I spotted Ludger, face down and blood running from a cut in his forehead. I massaged his face and neck with snow to bring him to and then we carried him into the school. He was okay. Many boys had lumps, cuts and bruises and the teacher was appalled at the extent of the injuries. She outlawed all types of warfare, threatening to call in our parents if necessary. She demanded more civilized games.

Challenged, we formed a small discussion group, a think tank of sorts, and tried to invent a new thrilling game that might meet her expectations.

It started out as relatively harmless play. One boy would stand on a small sled while a group would grab the towrope and race around the schoolhouse turning corners as fast and as sharply as required to send the passenger flying.

Then we got a larger sled with up to six passengers and more than a dozen racers at the towrope; the aim was to dump the whole load helter-skelter on a sharp corner turn. That time I was with the passengers. We stayed on after the first turn. The sled picked up speed and, at the second turn, we went flying as the sled sped on.

Five of us got up, one stayed down. Obviously, Aurèle Thériault was in pain. We reached down to help him to his feet but he screamed for us to stay away from him, not to touch him. We were puzzled. The girls gathered around, some were crying; then, the teacher came up.

"It's a broken collar-bone," she said.

She directed us to stretch him out on the sled and, with a scarf, she tied his arm to his chest.

"Take him home," she ordered.

Edgar, Aurèle's brother, and I pulled the sled. After a few minutes we reached the blacksmith shop. Jack spotted us. He hurried to the road, looked at me and grinned.

"Glad to see it's not you this time. Who's he and what happened?"

I told him part of the story.

"Wait here," he said.

Harry was hitched in no time. Jack spread out a deep bed of fresh straw in his large sled and he picked up the little sled, with the accident victim immobilized in it, and place it on board. The snakewhip cracked and Harry went galloping towards Aurèle's home.

I continued on my way and, as I went past the store, Dad spotted me.

"How come you're home so early?"

I told him the whole story. He looked at me intensely and I expected him to say something but he remained silent. A few minutes later, he left to see my cousin.

The next morning, my father hitched his horse to the sleigh and off he went to the Chatham hospital, once again pressed into ambulance service.

A few days later, I was called into his office for a private talk. He spoke in a low voice. He told me that the school kids were playing rough and dangerous games and that he suspected I was the instigator and promoter of most of them. Gradually he raised his voice as he warned me to mend my ways or else he would teach me the lesson of my life.

Head bowed, I listened. I had to change.

The store had just been stocked with a new batch of Christmas toys. Those left over from previous Christmases had also been brought down from the second floor. I did not want any of the toys; what I wanted was a brown leather schoolbag that had been in the store for months – the one with an engraving of a bucking bronco.

"It's very expensive and I don't believe we can afford it," Dad said.

I didn't like the old canvas bag with the narrow canvas strap that cut into my shoulder. I felt I had the right to express my opinion on the choice of a useful Christmas gift.

November 29 was my birthday. That evening, after homework, Mom told me that Dad wanted to see me at the store. I ran over and he greeted me with his best smile.

"I have something here for you as a birthday gift. Happy Birthday!" And he handed me the bucking bronco leather schoolbag. My eyes filled with tears of joy, I thanked him profusely and gave him a kiss. Walking on a cloud, I headed for home on the double.

It was pitch dark outside, the yard had a little snow and the rest was dark frozen earth. On the run I took a flying leap from the store entrance platform, skipped the three steps, hit on something that bounced me up in the air again and I landed smashing my face on the frozen ground.

At first, I couldn't see anything. Then, there was a ringing noise in my ears and a cascade of tiny lights blurred my vision. Slowly, I got up, still clutching my gift. I felt unsteady on my feet and had to wait for my vision to return. My nose was bleeding and I could feel a lump developing on my forehead. I was crying and laughing at the same time, the joy of the moment still with me.

Finally, I could make out a faint outline of my home. I staggered over and walked in. Mother, who of course knew of my gift, was waiting with the kids to share in my joy.

"My God! What happened to you?"

I couldn't answer.

She led me to the sofa and called the store. Dad came in immediately. Water was already boiling. There was blood all over my sweater, so he took it off gently and washed my face to evaluate the damage. He packed my nose to stop the bleeding and dabbed iodine on the abrasions on my face and hands. He took a silver dollar, applied it to the lump on my forehead and bandaged it in position. A piece of celluloid covered my broken nose for protection.

Then began the investigation. I gave my very mysterious version. He lit the lantern and went out to inspect the scene. Within minutes he was back. It seems that someone had left a sled on a patch of ice below the steps. I had hit that sled sending it flying and taking an almost fatal plunge.

The Bicycle
Roméo D'Amour

I never owned a bicycle; but at the age of eight,
I could ride one. There was only one type of bike in our
neighbourhood, the big one with a straight crossbar.
Some had a spotlight and a bell; all had a parcel carrier at the back. They were very heavy for a kid and
riding them was a feat.

You approached the bike from the left. You had
to twist yourself like a pretzel to get part of your
body under the crossbar and your foot on the right
pedal while your right arm was extended over the
main bar to reach the handlebars. In that most uncomfortable position, you had to pedal while maintaining enough equilibrium to effect the ride.

During this apprenticeship, you had to make sure
that, when off balance, the bicycle would lean to the
left. That way, in case of trouble, you would hit the
road standing up. If you went off balance to the right,
the crossbar would prevent you from taking correc-
tive action; the bike would fall away from you, with
you on top, where your shins would hit the sprocket
wheel and your mouth the crossbar.

Gliding was the best way to start. There was a slight incline between the store and the warehouses. I would take a bike (with or without the client's permission) and, with one foot on the left pedal, let it roll down the incline. That's how I learned to keep my balance and to steer the bike.

Pedaling was something else. After multiple spills, bumps and bruises, I earned a certain proficiency in the sport. Often, a store client, coming out to a missing bike, had the questionable privilege of seeing a twisted-up kid coming at him full speed to thank him for the joyride.

My father warned me that, in any event, I was bound to end up with a broken neck; either from a fall off the bike or from the punishment he would personally mete out should I damage a client's bicycle.

In 1925, we got a new teacher. She took room and board home. In addition to her good looks, there was something very special about this girl: she had a bike. It was comparatively undersize with no crossbar. I soon discovered that, by lowering the seat, I could ride sitting straight up, like a man. Dad warned me not to touch that bicycle, ever!

Nevertheless, I planned that, by hook or by crook, I would take that bike for a long ride. I had to bide my time but the opportunity arose at noon in late September.

"I forgot my lunch on the kitchen table this morning," I said. "If you allow me to take your bicycle, I could drive home, have lunch, and be back here for one o'clock."

She hesitated for a few moments, looked into my pleading eyes and gave in reluctantly.

"I'll lower the seat for you," she said.

"Oh, no. I can do it."

I rode more than a mile as happy as a competent pilot on his first solo flight. This was luxury, absolute opulence!

At ten to one, I was heading back, approaching Jack's bridge. I was coming down the steep hill at top speed, with reckless abandon, singing at the top of my lungs. The front wheel hit a pocket of soft sand and I lost control. The bike hit a fence post and I was hurled into the wire fence.

Quick as a cat, I scrambled to my feet and grabbed the handlebars. What a mess! The force of the impact had twisted the front end of the bike in such a way that the front wheel was almost against the seat. The frame was bent just below the steering post. It was major damage. I panicked.

"My God, why did you throw me against the wire fence? I should've been thrown into the river and left to drown."

I looked around. No one had seen me. I held the handlebars high and let the bike ride on the rear wheel. With a heavy heart, I made it back up the hill to Aunt Émilie's house. They hadn't finished their meal and were still sitting around the table, including Big Wilfrid. He was the man I wanted to see. My aunt sensed that I had a problem.

"Now, Roméo, tell me. Is there something wrong? You look so pale."

"I must talk to Wilfrid."

(Big Wilfrid was an ex-soldier. He got over to Europe too late to see action but with his regiment he had paraded in Brussels, for Albert I, King of Belgium. He had a picture to prove it.

Wilfrid was not only big, he was strong!

My Dad had witnessed a scene on the Hardwicke wharf where men were busy rolling gasoline drums up a ramp into a motor truck. The ramp was steep and the men were quickly exhausted from the effort; just then Big Wilfrid was walking by. In a loud voice, someone said:

"Now, if we had a strong man like Big Wilfrid here, we wouldn't have to slave like this. He wouldn't need a ramp. He would just grab the drum and lift it right up there into the truck."

They all laughed – not my Dad. He watched Wilfrid solemnly walking towards a drum that he tilted with his left hand; with his right hand, he grabbed the lower rim and lifted the 500-pound drum "right up there into the truck"

Wilfrid continued on his way. No one was laughing now.)

"I'll be with you in a minute," said Wilfrid.

The clock struck one. At school, lunch break was over. An eternity later, Wilfrid came out with me and looked at the bicycle.

"You could've killed yourself. Sure you're not hurt?"

"I'm okay but the bike's a mess," I answered. It was the first time I had spoken directly to the man.

"I'm not sure I have the tools to fix this. It will be difficult to unbend because this type of metal has a tendency to bounce back... Let's see... I'll start by removing the wheel and the handlebars... I guess I'll have to take out the steering post..."

I kept thinking, "Why doesn't he use those big powerful hands to straighten out this disaster. A miracle is what I need now."

Out loud I said, "I'll wait."

"Look, my friend," said Wilfrid, "I have a two-hour job here, maybe more. Go to school and drop in on your way back at four o'clock. Maybe it'll be ready by then."

My heart sank. There was to be no miracle. But I wasn't about to tell the truth to the teacher. I wanted a big lie to make it look right.

I mumbled to the worried teacher that the front wheel had jammed.

"Incredible! A new bicycle."

At four o'clock, I was the first one out of school. I ran like a scared rabbit to Aunt Émilie's.

"Where's Wilfrid?"

"What's the big rush? He's in the shed," answered my aunt.

There was the miracle of miracles! The bike was like new. Wilfrid just stood there marveling at all that happiness in me. I almost got down on my knees to thank him.

"Dad will pay you whatever it cost," I promised.

"Don't worry kid, it didn't cost anything, only my time; and my time is my gift to you."

Then I understood that this Big Angel was not going to tell my Dad.

"How come the handlebars are lower?" inquired the teacher.

"Oh, I'll take a wrench and adjust them," I offered.

"Don't bother," she said.

Dad decided to give me certain responsibilities that were meant to assist him with the chores and to try to instill a certain degree of discipline in my daily life.

In the boys' bedroom, above the kitchen, my bed was near the stairway. Next to the bed was a large window facing east to a startling view of the river and the bay. Wake-up time was six o'clock. I always knelt at the same spot for my morning prayers, facing the window and the water. Here was the ever-changing view, from the serenity of a glorious sunrise to the fury of a stormy sea. My fascination with the sea often caused an interruption in my prayers. But soon I was ready to start my day.

I had to light the wood stove. Mom would be up in 30 minutes and the stove had to be humming by then. I always prepared a good supply of dry wood and kindling the day before. It took me about five minutes to have that happy fire going.

Then, I helped with the barn chores. That meant I had to water and feed the horse and the cows, and clean the barn. I would return to the house, wash up, change clothes, and eat a hearty breakfast. By then it was time to go to school.

At half past four, I was back from school. We were allowed one hour to play and for supper. After the meal, I would fetch the cows and take them into the barn for milking. I would then water and feed the horse, cows and pigs. My next jobs were to refill the wood box and prepare kindling. Time was scheduled for study and homework and, at nine, we were sent to bed after kneeling by that window facing the sea to recite, with some distraction, my evening prayers.

Mack, our horse, had his own idea of fun. We could take him to the barn but he would balk at the door refusing to go in. Every time it was a major effort and, usually, we ended up angry with him. One afternoon, as we were coming back from school in the buggy, in heavy rain, Dad announced:

"From now on, Mack is going straight into the barn. Enough foolishness."

We got home and unhitched Mack. Dad stripped the horse of his harness, collar and bridle, leaving only the halter. He led the horse to the barn door where Mack again played delaying tactics.

Dad gave me one end of a long sturdy rope and tied the other end to Mack's halter. He went in the barn and made one loop around a post by the stall.

"Hold that rope tight," he said.

He picked up the whip and let go with a mighty whack. Mack almost pulled the rope out of my grip and shot in like a bullet. Never again did that horse pause at the barn door.

Our cow, Brindle, also had her own personality. She would come into the barn and then refuse for a good while to enter her stall, a major waste of time for me as, by that time, I still had studying and homework to do. I complained about this to my father; mother added it caused her a waste of time also, it delayed milking time.

"Tomorrow afternoon, I'll straighten her out for you," he said.

Next day, when I took the cows to the barn, Brindle entered without hesitation and then proceeded to wander around close by her stall. I tried to coax her in, she refused. Dad was there, watching. He came over and grabbed the cow by the horns to pull her back and set her right. Fighting back, she shook her head and smashed his knuckles against the pole. He muttered a quick curse and twisted her neck so fast, she flipped on her back. Flexing his fingers and nursing bloody knuckles, he went back to the store.

I reported the scene to Mom.

"I think Brindle got the idea, now," she said.

And so it was.

One day in March 1925, I came home from school early. I was sick again. Violent headaches would last for hours and turn my stomach.

"I think your appendix is acting up," remarked my father when he came back from the store to check up on the reason for my early return.

Mom gave me a pillow and a blanket. I stretched out on the living room sofa and slept for about an hour. I woke up feeling better.

At six o'clock, my Dad came in for supper.

Just as we were sitting down, the door flew open and in barged Camil, out of breath, and with an expression on his face that told of a tragedy. He spoke loud and fast. In short, jerky sentences.

"My son Placide was shot in the head. He's bleeding bad. Maybe, by now, he's dead!"

My father pushed back his chair, got up quickly, grabbed his coat, hitched Mack to the buggy; and, with Camil babbling away, went racing up the river road, half a mile past our little schoolhouse, mud and slush flying.

When they got to the house, Placide was in bed, his face a bloody mess. Dad washed away the blood and immediately realized that, for once, excitable Camil had not exaggerated; the boy's left eye had been smashed by a bullet.

With the nearest doctor 30 miles away, my father was often called upon to act as a doctor's substitute to provide first aid treatment. Also, because he was Justice of the Peace, he questioned witnesses to establish circumstances related to incidents or accidents.

Eventually, he got the story straight.

William, Placide's older brother, had taken the gun and yelled to Placide that he was going to shoot the dog. Placide came on the run and, as he was rounding the corner of the house, William fired the shot.

It was early evening when Dad returned.

"Get ready for eight o'clock tomorrow morning. I'm taking Placide to the hospital and you're coming along to have your appendix removed."

That morning it was snowing heavy wet snow, the roads had become almost impassable. The horse was forced to a walk. The trip lasted several hours. At the hospital, Dr. McKenzie scheduled Placide for emergency surgery. My turn would come the next morning.

When I was wheeled to the operating room, I spotted Placide and waved to him. He waved back. Some minutes later, a mask was pushed over my face and I choked on chloroform. I tried to wiggle away but firm hands held me still and I drifted off to sleep. I woke up happy to be alive. Pain wasn't the problem but the lingering taste of chloroform nauseated me.

I could not eat. The first meal came up, tomato soup. I hate tomato soup. I can't even stand looking at it. I left it there and, since I could only speak a little English, I couldn't explain myself. They drew their own conclusions. Two nurses came over and poured the lukewarm abomination in a kettle-like container. One nurse held my head steady while the other forced the spout into my mouth and poured away. Gagging, I threw up. It was a disaster for the bed sheets and the nurses' uniforms. One of them slapped me and walked out of the ward.

My father had returned home but he had promised to be back in two weeks. The next day, they came with another unpalatable treat, cream of corn. They got the same scenario as the previous day. I felt exhausted and very depressed. Time passed slowly but one week after my operation, I was allowed to get up. It took me two days to get my weak legs in condition for a cautious walk to visit Placide who was slowly coming back to health.

No one else in this hospital could speak French. It was a bit unsettling when, Sunday morning, a nun came over to escort me to the chapel. Possibly because of my bad reputation with the nurses, my escort piloted me along by tugging at my shoulder. I knelt down and started to pray as well as I could, given the circumstances. The nun nudged me.

"Where are your beads?" she asked.

"My what?"

"Your beads."

I couldn't understand what she was talking about.

(Long after this incident, when I had time to reconsider, I realized that English wasn't very difficult to learn because many of the words are very similar to French. For example the word "rosary" is like "rosaire", easy to make the connection and understand. However, "beads" like our word "chapelet" are very different and do not lend themselves to simple extrapolation.)

She searched my pockets and came out with a key chain with a shiny slab in which was embedded a scene from some south sea island; it had been given to me by my brother Cyrille when, coming in from Newcastle on Friday, he had spent an hour with me. Angrily, the nun trotted me back to my bed table and looked in the drawer. I still didn't know what I was expected to find. Right away, she spotted the rosary, yanked it out and slapped it in my hand.

"Here are your beads, stupid."

She could have prevented this regrettable scene if only she had used a simple synonym. Now I was fighting mad. I pretended to pray, all the while reciting as in a litany:

"You sonavabeads! You sonavabeads!..."

One day, ages later, Dad came to the hospital to pick me up. We had a marvelous lunch at the Riverview Hotel. To me, Chatham, a town of about 2000 people, was a big city full of glamour and wonderful sites.

In the afternoon, we visited Jack Carvell, the horse trader. There were some two dozen horses for sale or trade and I was afraid Dad would be tempted to trade Mack. As the men looked over the horses, I sat in Mr. Carvell's office and admired a series of colored pictures of famous racers. The great Dan Patch held center spot on the wall where the King, the Prime Minister or the Pope should have been. After a while, Dad came back. He hadn't traded Mack after all.

We went to the Premier Café, a Chinese restaurant, for steak and fried onions. We returned to the hotel for a short break and then off we went to the cinema, my first movie – silent movie, of course. I faintly recall the title: "A Fight on the Panama Canal". What a fight! What a movie!

Back to the hotel, I had problems going to sleep as I relived the memorable events of the day.

General Cambronne

Ludger D'Amour

My paternal grandfather joined the French Navy at 14 and, for a few years, underwent rigorous training in seamanship. That, I suspect, would account for his strong sense of discipline. My father's upbringing, along with his own experience with the Coast Guard, kept the tradition very much alive. So, inevitably, our clan learned early the importance of a clearly spelled out code of conduct and discipline.

I was the 5th child of a family that was eventually to total 17 (eight girls and nine boys). Early in life, we learned about sharing Mom's tender loving care. For Dad's attention, we would line up for a lively dance around the room or to sit on his knees for a happy song. We would also be singled out individually to tell of our day's adventure.

No toy was ever exclusively mine to own. Even my clothes could be transferred to a sibling should the need arise. But ours was a happy home and, after more than 70 years have passed, the bond is still strong among those of us who remain.

We were never poor. Food was excellent and plentiful. Clothing adequate and clean. Our house was roomy, modestly furnished and comfortable.

Mealtime was always special. One of us, the star of the hour, would tell a happy tale about a recent experience and, towards the end of the evening meal, our love of music transformed this joyous crew into a disciplined choir singing old French and English songs. It was the perfect spawning ground for the storytellers and music lovers we all became.

We often went to the store where Dad worked – possibly because he wanted to give Mom a well-deserved break. Whenever we were there, Dad would monitor carefully the conversations between customers and pay close attention to the topics discussed.

Many of the regulars came over for lack of better things to do. In winter, they would sit around the stove smoking slow deliberate puffs on their pipes, generating rich aromas from their Master Mason, Long Tom and Rosebud choice tobacco. Some chewed tobacco lustily and long jets of dark brown stain would hit the stove to create spit-and-fizzle sound effects.

There was a lot of talk about politics. Dad subscribed to three French and three English newspapers and long sessions would be spent discussing the news. Many of the men had served in the First World War of 1914-18 and could contribute unique insight on some of the international events.

My father was pleased to see us taking an interest in the news, in the political discussions and the occasional impromptu debates. He was on the alert whenever one of our local standup comics took center stage. If the performance seemed to drift into uncharted territory, he would discreetly let us know it was time to leave.

The vocabulary in usage at the time was clearly classified. There were words for polite conversation, neutral words and some – almost daring – that could be tolerated in certain circumstances. Some words were never acceptable. Home, our language was to reflect high moral standards and correct upbringing and, for a while, childish innocence protected us from the forbidden vocabulary.

When I was about five years old, I discovered a gem of a word. A word my grandfather used effectively in certain situations. A word that seemed to express clearly and forcefully one's frustrations. That word was *Merde!* (Shit!).

Years later I found out that there existed an officially accepted euphemism (in French): *Le mot de Cambronne.* But at the time, I hadn't read the great Victor Hugo and thus was unaware of General Cambronne's exclamation of frustration at the turn of events during the Battle of Waterloo.

Lacking this bit of historical trivia and as I was on the losing side of an argument with my sister Geneviève, I said "*Merde!*"

Quick as a flash, Dad picked me up from behind the table, carried me airborne over everyone, and gave me a slap on the bum. He then took me to the living room, left me on the sofa and closed the door. He hadn't bothered to provide any explanation no doubt thinking that, if I was precocious enough to use that kind of vocabulary in context, I was smart enough to know what I was saying.

I cried my little heart out, drenching a yellow sofa cushion in the process, and then I fell asleep. When I woke up, the sun was shining; I felt refreshed as nature after the rain. From the kitchen, I could hear my mother singing as she kneaded the bread. Quietly, I went to join her.

"Ludger," she said, "if you had a hat, I could take you to church with me next Sunday."

Mother was a good diplomat and instinctively she knew this was a good way to provide Dad with an opportunity to make amends. We weren't taken to church often before we made our first communion; I liked the outing and loved the suggestion that I might get a boater hat.

There were several hats in the store but only one I liked. It was made of fine yellow straw with a slightly rolled brim and it sported a blue ribbon with gold letters. I loved that hat!

Now, I felt it was up to me. Timidly, I entered the store where my father was busy with a customer. I went over to the glass case where the hats were displayed. Dad stopped what he was doing, came over, picked me up and sat me on the counter. His eyes were pools of kindness. He reached behind the case, picked the boater hat, placed it at an angle on my head and adjusted the elastic band under my chin. Then, he stepped back to admire the effect.

I was on top of the world. I had a new hat. And I knew my Dad loved me.

Man Overboard

Ludger D'Amour

Somehow, we got Mom to agree to let Cyrille, Roméo, Maurice and me go with Dad and five other men to Burnt Church. It was 1923. I was about six years old. A cousin of ours, Lionel Schofield, was also on the trip. Six men and five little boys on a 15-mile crossing of the mouth of the Miramichi river from our home in Baie-Ste-Anne.

The men were going to see W. B. Snowball, our local Member of Parliament to get a wharf built at Eel River Bridge. Mr. Snowball was at his summer home in Burnt Church. The men were in a good mood. To them the trip had the right mix of pleasure and important business. There was Damase Arseneau a WWI veteran decorated for bravery, Évé Thériault my father's cousin and owner of the boat, Edmour Thériault another cousin, Henri Schofield my god-mother's husband, Will Savoie the liberal party organizer, and my Dad who was to act as the official spokesman for the delegation.

It was a 24-foot boat with a small cabin up front and a single-piston 5-hp engine that couldn't quite bring the boat to a cruising speed of five knots. We had a generous supply of cookies and soft drinks. The men had other supplies in the front of the cabin, a cache out-of-bounds to the kids.

After a few hours of the best trip ever, we docked at an imposing wharf facility. To our way of looking at the world, Burnt Church took on airs of Acapulco. We got off the boat and went to see the Indians who were making baskets at the edge of the reserve near the wharf. We were free from adult supervision. The men strutted about with big rolls of blue papers. Everyone spoke English. It was definitely a momentous occasion.

I was so taken up by all these new experiences that it took me some time before I looked over and realized that my home was out there somewhere across that great sea. We followed the men to Mr. Snowball's summer residence. The MP looked venerable with his snow white hair but the main attraction was his new car that we studied from all angles.

Madame Snowball insisted that we come up on the veranda and try out her swing made of net. Because she spoke English, I was intimidated; but, when she came to me with a handful of blue grapes, I knew we could become very good friends.

At noon they took us to a sort of hotel with big tables and plenty of utensils. The men were dressed up in their Sunday best, so they put napkins around their necks like when Mom puts bibs on us at home. We were served ribs of lamb, definitely not my first choice, but the gravy and potato more than made up for it. To complete the banquet, there was plenty of chocolate cake and milk.

When we came out of the hotel, a strong breeze was developing. As we were barefoot, off we went to run along the water's edge where the odd breaker would sometimes reach higher than expected. We had a great time!

However, things were beginning to sour. The wind got stronger and the waves livelier. Because they had kids with them, the men closed their meeting earlier than planned. They shook hands with Mr. and Mrs. Snowball and re-iterated the purpose of their visit.

We got to the wharf, bought a full tank of gas and set off for home. To us it was all fun. As the bay was menacing, we were told to stay in the cabin. We weren't worried because we knew the men had experienced worse weather. The sea got more rough and the boat rolled and pitched. We didn't seem to make much progress. Battering from the waves loosened the cabin walls and a board struck me on the head, not much damage, only a lump.

Then the fog rolled in. The motor droned on but steering was difficult. After a few hours, we came to a gully between the two islands at the mouth of the bay. Damase chose this moment to go for a bottle in the bow – I suppose he wanted to warm up the crew. He was crawling carefully, holding on to the unstable cabin wall, when the boat rolled and pitched, throwing him overboard. He disappeared!

Henri turned the boat around and the maneuver almost capsized us. We rushed out of the cabin. Damase couldn't swim but somehow he had made it back to the surface. Arms outstretched, his pipe held firmly in his front teeth, with every wave passing over his head he reappeared regularly drifting farther and farther away. Someone was desperately trying to untie the anchor rope for a lifeline. Henri was doing his best to keep the boat steady. The spectacle was fascinating. We weren't worried because we knew that every man on board could master the impossible. Moreover, Edmour was known to be an excellent swimmer.

Will threw the line, Damase grabbed it and held on. They pulled him on board. Even though he was deserving of another medal for bravery and endurance, he settled for a generous gulp of whiskey.

As we neared home, I noticed that Roméo and Maurice were somewhat pale and unsteady. I could feel a big lump where the cabin and I had met. But, in spite of everything or because of it, we were happy with our day of adventure and discovery. Before we got off the boat, the men made us promise not to mention any part of the events we had witnessed.

Six months later, Évé and Damase, having had a few too many on New Year's Eve, gave a detailed if somewhat confused account of our trip to Burnt Church. Mom and my godmother were surprised that kids our age could have kept such a secret for so long. In spite of our discretion, we were never again invited on outings with the men.

Some time later, the government built our wharf and Dad was the foreman.

The Dream

Ludger D'Amour

There was a hitching post in front of the store where Will Savoie would leave his mare while he spent hours in friendly conversation with my Dad. They were close friends. Will was rather short, bald and a little on the plump side. In my opinion, he was perfectly bilingual as he seemed to stutter with equal intensity in both French and English.

Whenever there was a lull in business activities, they talked politics or local gossip. Will and Dad would analyze each and every news item and editorial in the Saint John, Quebec City and Montreal papers that came home three times a week. On off days, local gossip took center stage. As Will was the organizer for the Liberal Party, politics was a clear area of complicity for the two men. Dad respected Will's knowledge of current affairs whether it was provincial, national, international issues. With their know-how and political contacts they made a formidable team.

One warm drizzly day, Will hitched his mare to the railing in front of the store and came in with a mischievous twinkle in his eyes.

"Antoine, I had a strange dream last night."

"I'll be with you in a minute," said Dad who was busy writing carefully in a large ledger. He put away his pen, dried the notations with a brand new blotter and replaced the large book on a shelf under the cash register.

"A political nightmare, I suppose."

"More like a story with a special twist."

They sat down in front of the stove where many a tale was told in the rich aroma of pipe tobacco. They were alone. I wished myself invisible and inaudible in the hope of being allowed to listen in on the conversation.

"I dreamt I had a fight with my neighbour."

Everyone in the area knew the man. His manners were rude and his rages fearsome. He could pick a fight with anyone, including mild-mannered Will.

"I don't know exactly how it happened," Will continued. "Somehow the rifle I had in my hands went off and I shot him. He died instantly. I was arrested, questioned, photographed and locked up."

I inched closer, the better to observe the expression on their faces while the story unfolded amidst stuttering and dramatic pauses

"I had to admit to everything. The trial was held with judge and jury. There were plenty of witnesses. The evidence against me was rock solid and overwhelming. I was doomed, I knew I would hang."

"It would be hard to get out of a mess like that," said Dad.

"That's when my lawyer suggested I plead mental incompetence. You know – cr-cr-cr-crazy!"

Dad was about to say something but apparently changed his mind. So, Will continued.

"My lawyer told me to try to find a reliable witness, someone who could vouch for me. Someone who would convince judge and jurors that in my past behaviour I had done things that would cast doubt on my mental condition. I told him you could do it.

"I said, Antoine D'Amour is a Justice of the Peace, a respected businessman and a good Christian. He's my friend and, right now, my best chance to escape the hangman's noose."

Dad didn't react.

"So, Antoine, you were called to testify. The Prosecutor asked you if you had noticed anything in the past that would indicate that I had mental problems. You were there, in front of the Court, the room was filled to capacity and my life depended on your declaration. You know that I trust you, Antoine, but you can understand that I was a little worried.

"But when you declared to the Court, 'Your Honor, I believe this man has been crazy for a long time', I breathed a sigh of relief."

"Then the Prosecutor asked, 'What makes you say that?'"

"You answered: 'It's been obvious to me for quite a while because that fellow should have been shot a long time ago.'"

Both men burst out laughing.

It was re-assuring for me to note that two grown men could still enjoy something as innocent as a dream.

The Main Event

Ludger D'Amour

Today, the village of Baie-Ste-Anne, New Brunswick, includes the three small villages of Eel River
Bridge, Manuel's Post Office and Baie-Ste-Anne. They
are Acadian communities, each with an important segment of immigrants from Les Iles-de-la-Madeleine who
had chosen to move to the mainland at the dawn of
the 20th century.

When I was a kid, each community was fiercely
independent and defended its territory aggressively.
Each group had its own champion and, when the occasion arose, he was expected to rise to the challenge.
Fights were so frequent that a section of the territory
where many confrontations took place, was known
as Quarrelling Hill.

I grew up in Eel River Bridge. There were many
things to keep us busy on our little farm. We had animals to take care of and there was firewood and kindling as part of our daily chores. Of course, whenever
a neighbour was in need we were expected to pitch
in. But we found time to play most of the games kids
our age played everywhere on the continent at the

time. However, this bucolic way of life could sometimes provide highly dramatic moments.

In 1927, I was 11 years old when my parents gave me permission to go listen to a fiddler at a wedding. I had to have supper at home first. Curfew was at dusk – it was October – not much time for a party. But because these occasions were rare, nothing could have kept me from the anticipated excitement. My brother Maurice came with me. A friend of ours, Alcide Gaudet, joined with us along the way.

It was not uncommon for strangers from Baie-Ste-Anne to come to the wedding party. I won't stretch the truth by saying they were welcome, but they were tolerated... if they followed a strict protocol. There was a predictable sequence of events where a boy from the Baie would ask a local girl for a dance and, then, equivocal body language would generate jealously. With home brew courage, a local boy would challenge the outsider. For us, this traditional confrontation was the main event in any wedding celebration.

By the time we got there, the meal had been served, the tables cleared and the party was in full swing. Laughter and fiddle music filled the air. The house had probably never hosted so many people and, because of the mild temperature, the doors were left wide open.

We stayed outside and looked in as dancers crowded the floor while Joe Martin the fiddler played from the stairway. Things were not the way they should have been. Everyone was civilized. As the minutes ticked by, I began to feel I was pushing the limits of "curfew at dusk". I began hoping for a fight that would automatically extend my leave. Who would blame me for being late if I had an epic tale to regale the whole family?

The party was on and our time was running out. Maurice and I consulted frequently. We watched the dancers hoping for more action than the elegant choreography of a Lancers' set.

Suddenly there was a bit of stir in the kitchen. Cyriac Gaudet stopped the dance and told the belligerents to leave the house. They dallied. In his capacity as bouncer, he escorted them to the door. The crowd followed outside and we joined them. This was what we were hoping for, a fight!

From where I stood, the scene was backlit by an oil lamp in the kitchen window. The crowd formed a 25-foot circle around the two men. I was right there, ringside. Maurice and Alcide no doubt had also found a good vantage point as Cyriac was Alcide's father, the Eel River Bridge champion.

This trial by fisticuffs served to underline the rules of protocol: if you show up uninvited to a party, you must show good manners. The men from Eel River Bridge will not be pushed around by ruffians from Baie-Ste-Anne or Manuel's Post Office. And any offense to the rules called for a dual.

Our champion against theirs. Joe, the outsider, measured 5 feet 11 inches and weighed 210 pounds; Cyriac, 5 feet 10 inches and 195 pounds. This would be a first rate fight.

Off came the suitcoats and the vests as the onlookers justified over and over again the position of each clan. The neckties were ceremoniously folded and placed with the vests. Cyriac took off his glasses. Both men rolled up their shirtsleeves. The crowd held its breath.

Coming out of nowhere, David, an elderly gentleman with more energy than good sense, jumped between the gladiators. He was 5 feet 7 inches and weighed 130 pounds. He had probably missed the prelude and there he was, in the limelight.

Flashlights were turned on the better to see how David would fare between two Goliaths. The little man was in shirtsleeves and gesticulating like a devil in holy water all the while pouring out a torrent of unintelligible words. Now the crowd had eyes only for little David.

David's wife, Clarisse, jumped into the ring much more quickly that her 5-foot 10-inch frame and 170 pounds would normally allow. She grabbed her husband by the suspenders, threw a sweater over his head and carried him, arms flailing, out of the danger zone.

There was a thunderous roar of laughter from the crowd. Joe and Cyriac were still face to face but the spell was broken. Everyone returned to the dance while the two men, trying to maintain a degree of dignity, picked up their clothes from the fence posts.

Past curfew, Maurice and I returned home with a tale that made my parents forget how late it was.

The Sentence

Roméo D'Amour

L'Assomption, **an Acadian insurance** company, had granted for several years many scholarships to children of members in good standing. As I was in grade seven, I was invited to report to school and sit down for two hours to write an exam designed to establish whether I could qualify to get on the list for the lucky draw. It was summer 1927, in early July on a very hot Sunday afternoon.

That morning, I had walked to church and back. My new shoes had worked blisters on my heels. When I got home I told my mother that I wasn't going to school for the exam, "and that is that!" Dad was within hearing distance and, apparently, he saw things differently; not only was I going to school, he was going to escort me there personally.

Our parish priest, Father Poirier supervised the exam. We were told not to sign our papers, instead we were assigned a sort of lottery number. I answered the test questions as well as I could because, even though I considered the whole exercise futile, I was too proud to settle for a mediocre performance. Finally the ordeal was over. Now I had to undertake the long walk home. I soon sat by the roadside, removed my shoes and socks and, dressed in my Sunday best, I walked home barefoot.

When I got home I expressed my feelings unequivocally to my mother.

"Next year I'll find a way to get out of that silly test that comes up in the middle of the summer to spoil my vacation." However, I did not add "and that is that", just in case...

All summer I was kept busy delivering groceries. I greatly enjoyed that work. Mack was a real racehorse and I loved him. My father had warned me never to use the whip on that horse.

"Swishing the whip is enough to get him at manageable speed", he had added.

I had a wagon full of goods and five addresses on my delivery list, the last one more than two miles up the river road. In addition to the box of groceries, that last call had a 100-pound bag of flour.

"Get a man to help you with this," said my father as we loaded the wagon.

It didn't happen as planned (now I know it seldom does). Anyway, when I got to my last call, I knocked at the door and waited for a couple of minutes. Finally, a lady opened the door.

"Is your husband at home?"

"No, he's away. Is there a problem?"

"There could be," I said, pointing to the flour bag.

"I'll try to help you with that," she volunteered.

I looked at her again, she was definitely very thin and frail-looking.

"That's okay. I can manage."

I dragged the bag to the back of the wagon, to the very edge. Then I inched it almost halfway out. It fell on my right shoulder and I worked until it was in balance. Then I staggered into the house and dropped it heavily on the floor. I sat on a chair and gulped down a glass of water offered by the woman. She was visibly worried. I convinced myself that everything was fine except for a slightly strained back.

Awkwardly, I climbed on board the wagon. Now I could head for home. With the whip, I made the swishing sound close to Mack's ear and he took off. After a minute or so, I brought the whip heavily on the horse's back. I almost flew out of my seat. Mack was going at an incredible speed and the bumps in the road were tossing the wagon up, down and sideways forcing me to hold on to the seat with both hands.

When the horse hit a stretch of fairly even and smooth road, I could let go of the seat to rein him in. I pleaded with him to take it easy and, after a while, I brought him to a full stop so that we both could come to our senses. When I neared the store, Mack was still wild-eyed, shaking and sweating. I let him rest again for some 15 minutes hoping he would stop sweating but that didn't work. I let him trot gently and we entered the driveway where Dad was waiting, sitting on the steps.

"I'll unhitch Mack," he said and walked over to the horse. "You raced him. You whipped him!" exclaimed Dad.

"No, I didn't whip him," I lied.

"Roméo, you are lying. I can see the trace of a whiplash right down his back."

Suddenly, I spotted the dark strip down his spine. I was dismissed. I felt a bit apprehensive as to my next encounter with my father, knowing how much he loved horses, Mack in particular.

Later that day, things were quiet at the store and I joined him on the steps. He didn't speak for a while and then he turned and looked at me.

"Tell me, Roméo, do you think Mack is a fast horse?"

"Dad, it was scary," I answered with genuine admiration.

He looked away and smiled.

Twice a week, I made the rounds to buy blueberries. I stopped at just about every house along the road on both sides of the river. I didn't get along very well with dogs and, whenever I spotted one, I'd call for someone to take care of him before I got off the wagon.

Carlo was the name of the dog at Dominique Thériault's place. I knew I had better look out for him because of the previous year's confrontation. That time, I had spotted him tied up in the shed when I went to pick up blueberries. He had barked and lunged at me, snarling. A rope held him back but he had kept up faking fits of rage. I saw an oar near the door; I picked it up and gave him a good whack across the ribs that sent him flying into the corner.

I smiled to myself as I recalled how I had shut him up.

Today at Dominique's place, I checked for the dog. He was nowhere to be seen, so I supposed that he was tied up in the shed. I got off the wagon and headed for the kitchen door. Too late, I saw Carlo asleep close to the basement wall, no more than 10 yards away. I was hoping to tiptoe to the door without waking him up, when I was attacked by a streak of black fur. Immediately I experienced what I had always dreaded, the jaws of a vengeful dog closing firmly on my leg. I leaped in the air and came down fighting, kicking and cursing at the mongrel with murder in my eyes and in my heart. The dog panicked and, as fast as he could go, he raced way up the plowed field before he paused to look back. I made a move towards him and he took off further again.

The kitchen door opened and there stood Dominique and the entire family.

"Did he bite you?"

"You're damn right he did, the sonovabitch!"

A drop of blood marked each of the six spots where a tooth had sunk in. There was no more bleeding. Dominique fixed me up with iodine and a bandage. When I returned to the wagon I looked back and saw Carlo still way out in the field waiting for me to drive off.

I will always be impressed with the fact that this mutt had waited one whole year to pay me back in kind; and how he had tricked me into coming within grabbing distance.

Two miles up a side road past Dominique's place there was a pile of logs. Dad asked Ludger and I to truck this home, making as many trips as necessary.

I took the larger end of a piece of lumber and Ludger, the smaller. But something was wrong. A large number of wasps were buzzing around trying to intimidate us. Ludger was worried. I checked the wood-pile for the nest, it had to be there, somewhere. I spotted it deep inside the pile. I backed out quietly to the road to think this one through and make a plan.

I felt that I had to get rid of these lethal insects and load up.

"We can't go all the way home empty-handed to tell everyone that a bunch of stupid bugs scared us off," I said as I picked up the whip. "I'm going to whip them up real good. You just watch me."

I attacked with a flurry of whiplashes. The wasps came out in great number and that encouraged me to keep up the attack. Soon there were hundreds of nasty bugs hovering above me. Then they started moving as a black cloud towards the road.

"Run, Ludger, run!" I screamed.

My warning came too late. Ludger's head seemed to disappear in the black fog of stinging wasps. I jumped in with him, arms flailing but they didn't want to bother with me. After an eternity, as if by command, they returned to their nest.

Ludger was in terrible condition. His face puffed up, his arms and legs turning red while a searing burning pain tortured him. I tried to comfort him, to no avail. I threw the timber in the ditch and whipped the horse to a full gallop.

Dad took care of poor Ludger as I unhitched Mack.

"Next time it rains enough to soak the wood, I'll go with you and set fire to the hive," Dad said.

Ludger suffered through days of unimaginable torment and every time I saw him I felt guilty, sorry for my recklessness. A week later the nest was burned and we came back with our first load of wood.

That same summer, on August 16, 1927, as I was leaving the house in search of adventure, a shiny black car entered the store driveway. It was our parish priest, Father Poirier.

"Good-day, Father," I said, trying a fast getaway.

"What's your name?"

"Roméo."

"You're the lucky one. You're going to college. Let's go and tell your dad."

I had won an eight-year scholarship. The entire family rejoiced. To me, it was bad news. I didn't care for college. I was happy at home. I loved my life in the most wonderful setting a young boy could ever hope for. I feared that gloom and sadness would be my lot from now on, at the Bathurst College, more than 100 miles from home.

My mother began preparing outfits for my ordeal. With indelible ink, she marked my clothes for the life sentence I was to serve.

College Days
Roméo D'Amour

We were assigned the rumble seat for a 100-mile ride to Bathurst, on a hot and dry September day. Father Poirier had offered to drive Cyrille and I to college. He had to go because his brother, who had spent the summer with him in Baie-Ste-Anne, was also a student at Bathurst College. The weather had been unusually dry for several days and we got to our destination covered and choking with dust.

I was impressed at the sight of that big yellow brick building but the thought of having to spend my next eight years there gave me stomach cramps. I was 12 years old, I would come out at 20 with a Bachelor of Arts degree. Cyrille was in his second year and tried to make me feel at home.

I wasn't about to co-operate. Every day he took some time to give me briefings on what to expect and how to react. I didn't want to listen, I answered only in monosyllables and he became discouraged with my negative attitude. Some tyrant had drawn up the daily program: we had to get up too early, we were herded to Mass, the food was terrible and the homework interminable. I even got to hate recess.

I was truly homesick for my Mom's love, and her cooking, and I longed for Dad's presence. Whenever my three sisters and three brothers came to mind, I'd cry my heart out. I missed good old Mack and the thrill of riding with him. The breakwater, my favorite playground, had no equivalent in this dull and dreary place; and the sea wasn't there to inspire my prayers. I missed my friends and my old school. I was heartbroken.

Then, suddenly and for no reason, the torture ended. No more agony and despair. I believe that something must have snapped as if the power line carrying memories of home had overloaded and blown a fuse. Alive and happy again, I became a new boy in a new world. And I didn't write home anymore, Cyrille did.

"Tell Mom I'm okay," was all he could get out of me.

On November 29, Cyrille came to me during the morning recess and wished me a happy birthday.

"In less than one month from now, we'll be home," he added.

I cringed. I didn't want my sentimental line repaired because I feared the agony of blowing another fuse.

But the arrival of December re-enforced the idea that I would be going home soon. I thought of Mom and Dad, I actually could see their faces. I tried to remember the features of my brothers and sisters but it was a difficult exercise, they were sort of out of focus; and, to my dismay, I couldn't remember all their names.

"Oh, my God! I'm about to return home and I've forgotten someone's name... and I'm sure that someone is important. How can this happen to me?"

That night, before falling asleep, I was determined to find that name. I had to calmly recite all the names over and over again and, after a while, it came to me: Ludger!

Ludger, the soldier who had joined the enemy ranks to fight that winter war; Ludger, who had taken all the stings from the wasps I had whipped up last summer; Ludger, who had been my lieutenant and companion in my wildest adventures.

Now I could focus again and go to sleep.

On a beautiful cold winter evening, we arrived home to a hero's welcome. For Cyrille it was a repeat performance; for me, it was a first. Dad was all smiles, proud of his boys. Mother's eyes were full of tears of happiness. My brothers and sisters treated us with some reverence. But a small voice warned me never again to get caught up in too much sentimental mush; so, I spent most of my time listening to music and reading. As much as possible, I kept away from my old schoolmates. Two weeks later, when it came time to leave, I was in full control of my emotions.

Summer 1928 came. I again delivered groceries and bought blueberries. I was determined to give Dad all the help I could. I worked hard and seriously for the entire two months and, never once, was I involved in one noteworthy incident.

In September, my program of studies introduced Latin and Algebra, two new challenges. I was getting good results and had thoroughly adapted to the routine.

The owners of the store complex decided to sell the property and the new owners wanted to run the business themselves; that meant that Dad had no more work. Our family returned to our grandfather's house while a new roomy home was being built across the road, on our land up the river.

Under new management, the store complex was not doing very well. No longer involved in running the store, Dad was busy getting the little farm going. It was hard backbreaking labour but everyone persevered. The little farm provided life's essentials and the growing family was happy.

At college, the following year started out well. I was involved in the debating team. Also, I was studiously learning music and soon qualified for fourth cornet with the college band. But my studies always came first and my marks were excellent.

In the early days of October 1929, while I was playing football, I felt sick and quit the game. Cyrille, sensing trouble, suggested that I go to the infirmary.

"I have a splitting headache, nausea and blurred vision," I told the priest.

He checked my temperature, no fever. I had to plead to get permission to rest in my bed in the dormitory. He gave me an aspirin and hinted that I was faking it. At six o'clock the next morning, I woke up feeling rested. I tried getting up and fell back on my pillow. I forced myself to get up and I collapsed on the floor. I was put back in bed and ordered to remain there.

The priest in charge of the infirmary came in 30 minutes later. Again he took my temperature, looked at the thermometer, and froze. He took another thermometer and the second reading confirmed the first. He took me to the infirmary in a wheelchair.

Aurèle Chevarie, a classmate, had been there for a few weeks. He was glad to have a companion in misery.

"I know what you have," he said.

"What would that be?"

"I have scarlet fever and, my guess is, that's what you have too."

"What does that mean?"

"It means you're stuck here for 40 days."

He was right, of course. And the management of

the college feared an epidemic as we were 280 boys in the place. I discovered the true meaning of boring quarantine because Aurèle soon left and I was alone for weeks, eating very little and getting weaker and thinner.

I finally beat scarlet fever and paid the price. I could hardly stand. Slowly, I exercised, mostly walking, until I could feel some improvement. I had a lot of studying to make up for also.

At the end of November, very close to my birthday, I developed a severe earache. I woke up in the middle of the night in distress, sometimes screaming with pain. I was given an effective painkiller and fell back to sleep.

Next morning, Dr. Véniot came to visit. His diagnosis, mastoid. It was imperative that I was operated immediately, my father was contacted. He told Cyrille to take the train with me to Chatham; he would race to meet us there. He was concerned because the surgeon, Dr. McKenzie, was en route from Mont-Joli with a new car that he had bought in Quebec City. The hospital had told my father that the doctor was expected home later that day.

Dr. McKenzie decided to operate immediately. I was chloroformed again and when I came to, I felt good, no pain... yet. My head was bandaged and there was a thick pad of gauze behind my left ear. I tried to move my head and experienced a sharp pain. I soon learned to use both hands to move my head, leaving my neck muscles completely relaxed.

On the third day, Dr. Mackenzie asked the nurse to remove the bandage. She started unwinding and, each time she got near my left ear, I would wince. The doctor took over and cut the bandages leaving only a dried up patch behind my ear. He carefully took hold of one corner and suddenly yanked away. There was more surprise than pain and blood flowed down on my shoulder.

"It looks good," said Dr. McKenzie. "Nurse, put a new bandage on this young man."

Two weeks later, just before Christmas, Dad took me home. The snow-covered roads were in good condition and he kept the horse at a fast clip. I got a very touching welcome – like someone coming back from the dead. With all the kind attention and Mom's cooking, I got quickly on the road to total recovery.

When Dr. McKenzie, on one of his series of house calls dropped in to see me, he diagnosed that all was well. I could even hear the tic-tock of his pocket watch when he dangled it close to my left ear. He was extremely happy because, as he told us, his first mastoid patient had died, the second one was deaf, I was the third!

The total costs of the operation, including the house call, was fifty dollars.

A few days later, I woke up in the middle of the night. There was a lot of commotion in the house and everyone was up looking out the upper bedroom windows towards the bridge.

"What's going on," I shouted from my bed.

"The general store is on fire," answered my sister, Geneviève.

I heard the door slam as my father took off on the run across the river.

"Will someone please help me, I can't get up," I pleaded.

Geneviève and Ludger got me up and they placed a chair by one of the windows where we were all gathered to watch the dramatic scene unfold one mile downstream. Mother was crying and we all had tears in our eyes.

"Relax, Roméo, I'll hold your head for you," offered Geneviève.

I felt frustrated because I thought I should have been down there with Dad. Soon, I was mesmerized as the blaze grew more fierce. The whole complex was a giant silhouette with a blazing backdrop. Dad had formed a bucket brigade. They were fighting to save the house. The store was a gigantic murderous bonfire. Boxes of ammunition on the shelves and in the backroom were exploding with machinegun chatter. Then the large kerosene drum caught fire sending giant plumes of flames into the night air. The powder keg exploded and one wall of the store came crashing into the fire, the other wall followed shortly after. For a moment darkness covered the spot where the store had been. It was only a matter of time before the large warehouse would light up. In less than an hour, the flames were brighter than ever destroying the two warehouses in an inferno of exploding gasoline tanks and smaller flashes of other flammable materials

The men managed to save the house.

We were all very sad. I was sick in my heart thinking of the beautiful complex and the wonderful world it had provided for my childhood adventures. Late in the afternoon, Dad returned home bitter and exhausted; and a much older, sadder man.

After the Holidays, we returned to college. My head was still wrapped up in bandages. The two months I had missed would hurt for a long time to come. Learning algebra was now an uphill battle.

Learning was further enhanced at home. My father was a very generous man. We were well housed, well fed and well dressed (for the times). And he was always attentive to the needs of our neighbours. If my mother thought he exaggerated somewhat, she never disapproved. She would smile and throw up her hands.

"Antoine, you know the old saying about giving the shirt off your back... I can predict it will happen to you some day," she told him.

Camil Chiasson was a well-known member of our community. He was a good man but somewhat excitable. He spoke loudly and was inclined to exaggeration. And, when he was excited, he was prone to some confusion.

At one time while with his boys taking in the hay, he had hollered from the top of the load:

"Placide, the cow is sucking the calf" (omitting to add or vice-versa).

If he was pressed for time he would take a long round about short cut, like the time he was reading the school board's financial statement in public:

"One hundred and some dollars and some cents; eighty and some dollars and some cents; forty and some dollars and some cents..."

He was interrupted by wild applause and he wondered why.

One late December afternoon, my father came home from the store where he had purchased much-needed personal clothes: one warm shirt, one pair of winter underwear and some heavy socks. He put them away in the bedroom.

In walks Camil Chiasson.

"Antoine, can I use your phone?"

"Go ahead, it's yours, Camil."

He made his call and accepted a cup of tea. Then he started to enumerate the problems he had as a buyer of smelt on the bay. The temperature was always below the freezing point and the high winds were threatening his very life.

"I'm not dressed for this job. My shirt is *fini!* My socks are full of holes and my underwear looks like cobwebs. I know I have no choice but, this time, winter will get me. I'm condemned to die like a smelt, frozen in the ice. You're looking at a dead man, Antoine, killed by the bay, murdered by the awful winds." He had tears in his eyes.

"Wait a minute, Camil."

My father hopped upstairs to his bedroom and was back in a moment with the new wardrobe.

"Here, Camil, pay me when you can."

"May God bless you, my good friend."

And Camil went out with his precious box of clothes leaving Dad happier than a lottery winner.

Mother burst out laughing. "I knew it, Antoine. You did one better than the old saying: not only did you give away your shirt, but you threw in your socks and your underwear!"

These were the lessons that no college could ever offer.

On Hard Times

Roméo D'Amour

We were ten children at home in September 1930. Cyrille was forever absent as he was already studying for the priesthood. I had five sisters: Geneviève, Thérèse, Maria, Antoinette and Albertine (Léola and Alida having died earlier). And I had six brothers: Cyrille, Ludger, Maurice, François, Charles and Albert. Mom had given birth to twins on July 5, 1929, a special way to start on her second dozen.

In 1928, my father's brother, Uncle Albert, who lived in the Magdalen Islands, had called to announce that his wife Imelda had given birth to twins and that they were named Antoinette and Antoine in his honour. Now, one year later, my parents were able to reciprocate and our twins were named Albertine and Albert.

Military like, Dad read out a duty roster every morning. It always began with the farm chores. The rest of the day was set for land clearing. We were shown how to work with the horse and scruffer, block and tackle, crowbar, pick, shovel and axe. The field was free of timber but dotted with stumps and fieldstones.

We piled the uprooted tree stumps at one end of the field and piled the rocks by the fence for later transfer. We worked like convicts and enjoyed every minute of it. At the end of each week, even though progress was slow, we looked back at the patch of cleared land and took pride in our achievement. It was enough incentive to spur us to greater efforts. For good measure, my father would make certain to thank and congratulate us periodically.

It took four years of hard work to clear a field about 500 by 1000 feet. One late August day, the work was declared completed and the next morning, we got ready to burn the stumps.

The entire family gathered and some of the neighbours joined us for a celebration of sorts. We had some kerosene, matches, picks and shovels. Once the fire got going, we were kept busy circling the blaze to prevent it from spreading to the wooded area. Garter snakes, disturbed by the heat would slither away and, when spotted, they were terminated.

The party lasted well into the night.

To keep up with the ever-growing demands of a large family, my father had learned many trades but they were not all income generators. Every Sunday at High Mass, he was director of ceremonies; his assistance was greatly appreciated by the parish priest, especially on occasions like the annual Bishop's visit. His job of Justice of the Peace was occasionally demanding but not much better income-wise as his church activities. He was one of the unpaid school commissioners and a much solicited Liberal party organizer. For a while, he earned a regular salary as general store manager and, irregularly, he would get temporary employment as a local contractor on government projects.

Mr. Thurber, the Public Works engineer, would request his services as project manager every chance he got. Dad was intelligent, resourceful and had a well-deserved reputation as an excellent foreman. In the summer of 1932, he got the contract to supply stone for the construction of a new breakwater near the bridge in Eel River Bridge.

I was hired as time-keeper at a rate of $1.50 per day. I had to keep work records for the 20 men and to tally the number of truckloads leaving the quarry. The workday was from eight to six. I was always thrilled by the dynamite blasts that highlighted each day.

The men worked very hard. No machinery was involved but a lot of brawn and a lot of brain as much skill and strength were required to get those rock slabs ready for loading. Then the men had to lift the heavy stones into the waiting trucks. The men joked and laughed throughout the day, one would have guessed they were on a sort of picnic. I was sitting up there on the edge of the bank, above the workers, and I felt useless and embarrassed.

After a couple of days, I asked my father if I could work with the men down in the quarry. I would still keep time and register the truckloads but I had to get involved because I felt humiliated.

"The work looks easy from up the bank but it's very tough. I only hire mature well-muscled men. A 17 year old college boy like you wouldn't last two days; and, you could get hurt," he remarked.

"I know I can do it. Let me try. Please."

He agreed reluctantly.

I bought a pair of cheap leather gloves and, the next day, I came down to work with the men. Everyone had a good laugh. One asked me if I had any particular requests for when they would take me to the hospital before the end of the afternoon. I started cautiously, selecting medium size stones, and I got used to evaluating the weight and gauging my limits. At noon I was very tired, only my pride kept me going. When I got home at 6:30, I couldn't eat supper. I threw myself on the bed and fell asleep immediately.

At six the next morning I could hardly move. I hurt everywhere: neck, arms, legs and back. I did some limbering up exercises and went downstairs to one of Mom's hearty breakfasts. The day would never end. Each hour brought me closer to total collapse, but I made it. The next two days were on-going torture, and then it was the weekend. After three weeks I was doing my day's work as well as anyone else. The gang accepted me as one of theirs. After eight weeks and several pairs of gloves, I was in peak physical condition. I felt healthy and strong. But it was time to return to Bathurst College where, after months of pencil pushing, my manly physique re-lapsed to that of a "college boy".

I had a busy academic program and my extra-curricular activities included the debating team, some tutoring to the younger boys and playing cornet with the band. The months went by fast and soon it was time for the Christmas vacation. When I got home, there was an addition to the family, the eighth boy, Some of us could not rejoice over this new arrival; it was the depth of the terrible economic depression. When I first spotted that week-old baby in the crib, I told him:

"Antonio, we could have done without you."

There was no gainful employment for me the summer of '33. Sadly, it was the same for everyone I knew. Determined to make the best of a terrible situation, I went back to farm chores and buying blueberries. And I would take the occasional day off.

My mother was involved in a bit of a barter trade with blueberries, strawberries, raspberries, oysters, smelt, and eel for butter, eggs, and vegetables. Very rarely, someone would bring yellow marshberries.

One day, Jean Arseneau, Edgar Thériault and I headed for Ward Lakes about three miles in the woods. We each carried a 2-gallon pail. We reached the clearing and gazed at two miles of flat lands with twin lakes almost touching each other. We started walking on that soft, wet, spongy swamp land and, after a while, we reached the yellow marshberries. It was scarce picking.

"It's much better on the other side of the lake", said Edgar. "Let's go across from here."

I took a long pole to test the depth of the water under that growth; the pole went all the way down and never touched bottom. The idea of running 50 yards on this loose mushy carpet that was full of holes gave me goose pimples.

"Couldn't we walk around?" inquired Jean.

"That's at least a four-hour walk," said Edgar.

"We each have a handful. Let's eat them here and go back home."

Edgar didn't answer. He took off like a sprinter, dodging the holes and hardly touching the ground. In moments he was on the other side.

"They're plentiful here," he reported.

"Of course, no one wants to cross over," I shot back.

Suddenly, I found myself on the run, wide-eyed, holding my breath and dodging the holes with Jean right behind me. In seconds we were in the land of plenty and we got down to serious picking.

"Maybe we shouldn't think of that now," said Edgar, "but we'll have to go back carrying a pail of berries."

In an hour our pails were brimful of beautiful yellow marsh berries. Again on an impulse, I rushed across the swampy crossing, hopping as lightly as I could, my pail held high and a prayer on my lips with Jean and Edgar close behind. We were soaked with sweat, the emotional strain had sapped our strength but we were headed back. We still had a large swamp to cross, and over three miles of forest and two miles of road to walk before reaching home. After a while we noticed that the content of the pails had gone down some three inches.

"Another one of nature's mysteries," said Edgar. "The farther we walk, the less berries we've got in the pail and the more it weighs."

We got home a bit late for supper. I gave Mom my harvest and headed upstairs to bed saying:

"Whenever someone comes here to barter or sell yellow marsh berries, please be very generous."

How I Discovered Electricity
Ludger D'Amour

Growing up in the country, I learned about oil lamps and wood stoves. I also learned about the muscle power of men and horses. That was the extent of my knowledge about light and energy. In 1933, there didn't seem to be much work for anyone, I was 16 with an unfinished grade seven, so I didn't have a hope.

Someone in government borrowed from the USA the idea for the Relief Camp Project. A concept that appeared aimed at enlisting young men to do some land clearing. The work conditions were as bad as could be imagined by a committee of politicians and bureaucrats: room and board, dress in leftover uniforms of WWI and a salary of four cents per day.

I considered the idea.

"That isn't a decent way to start out in life," said my father. "It's degrading, it's a form of slavery."

I had to agree, but I wanted to start making my way, learn a trade, follow-up opportunities, join a business venture, or tackle the meanest task. There was no easy access to the mighty Canadian dollar. Anyway, it seemed to me that even prestigious labels such as "business venture" seemed to transform themselves into "meanest task".

There were some door-to-door peddlers who looked like they were making a living, some even drove cars. The Telegraph-Journal ran an ad for Fuller Brush salesmen. With more optimism than good sense, I applied. The Moncton office sent me a sample case and a list of sales tips.

I owned a shabby and fragile bike with wooden rims. I couldn't undertake long rides throughout the region on that contraption. I went to Newcastle to trade the wreck for a new sturdy CCM with double bars, double handlebar and a deluxe saddle, all for $40. They offered $5 for my old bike but I still couldn't come up with the $10 down payment. My friend Alden Assouf loaned me the money and I embarked on a five dollars per month payment schedule.

On bicycle I started out in life as a Fuller Brush salesman. I pedaled uphill and downhill, upwind and downwind, in fair or foul weather, everyday on abominable roads. In this business venture I experienced fatigue, hunger, deception, rejection, fear and dog bites. With my 25-lb sample case attached to my baggage carrier, many things came my way; however, I did not meet financial success.

I started my business in late August. That year, autumn quickly gave way to winter and the orders I had taken three weeks earlier had to be delivered by horse and sleigh. Our country roads in winter were always practically impassable; my chances were nil in Baie-Ste-Anne, so I decided to try my luck in Newcastle.

My father was a friend of Charlie Assouf, a businessman of Syrian descent who had married a Scottish lady and ran a store in Newcastle. They offered me room and board for $3 a week, one of their many ways to practice charity. They lived in a comfortable apartment above the store, and they had electricity!

I was amazed when I saw them light up the dark 15-step stairway by pressing a button. I noticed another button nearby which would pop up when the light came on. Logically, at the top of the stairs, a similar system worked the same way. I thought that was wonderful. To my satisfaction, it worked every time I tried it.

At the time, the complex system of wiring and switches hidden in the walls was a mystery to be pondered, not explored.

There was a hole in the wall in the kitchen where Mrs. Assouf inserted two metal claws to warm up her iron, another wonder. That, and the buttons for light, made this first day at Assouf's a time of delightful surprises. In less than an hour, I had learned a lot about Edison's magic wall system.

After supper, Mrs. Assouf got me to play a few games of Casino, my pension supplement, I supposed. I was very tired from that 35-mile bicycle trip and was eager for a good night's rest.

Alden, the young fellow who had financed the purchase of my bicycle, was their only child. He showed me to the bedroom. He walked in ahead of me, pulled on a chain and *Voilà!* Another way to turn on the lights.

Alone in the room, as I stripped down to my longjohns, I wondered how in the world I could turn that light off with something as unmanageable as a flimsy chain.

On the bed, standing on my suitcase, on tip-toe, I tried every method I could think of to push that chain back in the hole.

"This is stupid. Why not use the saner pushbutton technology?" I wondered.

Then I heard someone at the door. I fumbled, fell on all fours and found myself in the dark unable to understand what had happened. Convinced I had broken something, I slipped under the blankets.

Alden came in, pulled on the chain, the light came on – nothing broken.

"I thought you'd be sleeping by now," he said.

I mumbled a non-response and tried to keep an eye on the bulb swinging back and forth above me. A few minutes later, Alden reached up, pulled on the chain – total darkness!

Even though I was extremely tired, I couldn't sleep for some time as I marveled at the mysterious ways of electricity.

The following days confirmed the reliability of these strange inventions. It worked again and again.

And it still works.

Higher Learning

Roméo D'Amour

College life got more interesting. My marks
in English, French and Latin were very good. Greek
was more of a challenge but I was getting by better
than average. My performance in mathematics had
improved and I was now confident that my overall
results would be very honourable. I was starting the
last two-year stretch, which meant that Philosophy
would be taught and discussed exclusively in Latin,
no French or English allowed.

I was good in Latin but the thought that one would
have to study, analyze, discuss and debate only in that
language was somewhat daunting.

I had studied with interest, and in Latin only,
Julius Caesar's accounts of his wars in Gaul; it was
interesting and factual (one would hope). I followed
attentively his legions on the march across western
Europe; so, three years earlier, I had already mastered
reading Latin as easily as Sir Walter Scott's English
or Victor Hugo's French. Cicero had further raised my
interest in Latin texts with some of his speeches; I

particularly enjoyed his classic speech when, in the Roman Senate, he accused Senator Catalina of conspiracy and treason.

If I found pleasure in reading Julius Caesar and Cicero, I expected Philosophy in Latin to be drier and tougher to understand and discuss than reports on a military campaign or the indictment of a traitor.

So I started timidly on the road to Philosophy in Latin. I loved the courses and the last two years were, by far, the most enjoyable of the eight-year sentence I had received as a twelve year old country boy.

In February, 1934, I got a letter from my mother announcing the birth of a healthy little girl, the sixteenth! She was named Julie after my maternal grandmother. I think that we were resigned to an ever-expanding family circle and everyone saw her as a ray of sunlight in an otherwise dull world.

In June, 1935, I received my Bachelor of Arts degree, *cum laude*. I was worried because we were in the middle of the Great Depression; professionals like doctors, lawyers and engineers were out of work or busy working for nothing. Canada and the USA were on the ropes. Only Italy under Mussolini and Germany under Hitler seemed to be going places.

I tried to get financial assistance to return to university and study Law. Of course, in those times there were no government programs and I didn't know anyone who would help me along. Loans were never available to the poor – obviously the role of the banks was to bleed the country and not invest one red cent on improving the lot of the citizens.

I decided to enlist in the Navy. The system was still very much under British traditions and, with my name, I wasn't taken seriously. Still, they managed to slam the door in my face when they advised me that, in the unlikely event that I would be accepted, I would be required to fork over $280 to cover the cost of my uniform.

Father Gallien was our parish priest. One day he called me to say that he had found me a job in Montreal as professor at the Jean-de-Bréboeuf College. I was told to leave immediately and report to Father Lanteigne, his cousin who was a professor there at the time. Mom packed a generous lunch box, I picked up my little metal suitcase and Dad got me a one-way train ticket.

Father Lanteigne was puzzled, he had never invited me to come to the Jean-de-Bréboeuf; it was apparent to both of us that I was a sort of hot potato dropped in his lap by his wily cousin.

"I just don't know how to handle this situation," he sighed. "Don't be surprised if you have to go back home."

"Father, I'm a thousand miles from home and I have no money, not one cent!"

First he found me a room. Then he negotiated with the Director of Studies to let me have my meals with the teaching staff until someone could rule on my status. It only took a few hours, for me an eternity.

"We'll work something out," said the Director.

The next morning I was hired under contract for ten dollars every two weeks plus room and board. I was overjoyed to find myself in a very good room with a large window over-looking a wooded park. I had a single bed, a workdesk, a lamp, two chairs, a bookshelf and a sink. The food was abundant and excellent.

I was to teach English (second language) in grades eight, nine and ten. After a few weeks, I started giving tutorials to the many students in need of special coaching; and this paid the unheard of amount of one dollar per hour! Within two months I was making

$60.00 per month in addition to the $20 paid by the college. I bought myself a beautiful $17.00 radio and went to the movies every second Saturday.

It was a good year.

It was a difficult milieu, Jean-de-Bréboeuf College. It was college for the elite, the upper crust of Quebec society. Our students were sons of rich and influential people: judges, political leaders, doctors, dentists, engineers, merchants and other businessmen.

In the middle of the Economic Depression, most of the students from grade 12 up had their own cars and many were shiny new convertibles. The kids were intelligent, carefree, well dressed – Pierre Elliot Trudeau (future Prime Minister of Canada) was one of my students at the time – but the weak point was classroom discipline.

In September, 1937, I was assigned to teach English and Latin. My regular pay was doubled to $40.00 per month and tutorial rates went up to $1.25 per hour.

In early October, some of the teachers were experiencing great difficulty managing their classes, three of these were Jesuits. My personal background was stamped "discipline" all over. My father was a kind and just person but he would never have allowed a challenge to his authority. My eight years at Bathurst College had drilled a military type discipline in me. Half of the Eudist priests were ex-French Army World War One veterans. Our Director, Father Quelo had been a Captain in the infantry; he had been wounded five times and had been awarded eight medals for bravery on the battlefield – not the type of individual you want to stand up to.

In Bathurst, the end of recess was determined by two short whistle blasts that brought 280 students in a straight line, two abreast. The kids were marched to their classrooms. Instant obedience was the norm: the ringing of a bell, a blast from a whistle or a clap of the hands – there was order in the house.

I recall telling my father about a rebel student who had been dismissed. Visibly upset, he had said:

"Roméo, if you're expelled from college for misconduct, don't come home. Go West!"

So, the choices were there: push a pencil or rope a steer.

The situation at Jean-de-Bréboeuf had me worried. Keeping control in those classrooms was somewhat like walking a tight rope. I knew I had the skills for this job but I doubted my endurance.

One afternoon, as I was leaving my Latin class, I spotted Father Boutin at the door of a classroom where the students were having a ball. I walked over. I could see the teacher, at his desk, crying.

"They wouldn't do that to me," I said.

Late that evening, Father Boutin knocked at my door.

"I'm just back from a meeting where we discussed the debacle this afternoon. We need a strong arm for that group and I recommended you for the job."

I took my time to think this one over. He waited, in silence.

"Father, I accept the responsibility if you accept my two conditions: first, whatever I do, you approve; second, in my class, my word is law."

"Agreed," said Father Boutin.

We shook hands and he left. I sat at my desk in deep meditation.

The next morning, Father Boutin introduced me to my new class and left, rather in a hurry I thought. It was an exceptionally quiet day. It turned out to be a very quiet week. Friday afternoon, as I was getting ready to go down town, I met Father Boutin.

"You had a good week, Roméo," he said. "It's to be expected with that group but I don't think it can last; sooner or later, the more frisky elements will want to test you."

"I'll put it to you this way, Father," I answered. "Frisky, I don't mind; ornery, I won't tolerate."

One rainy morning, I could feel a change. As I was working at the blackboard, one of the bigger fellows at the back of the class threw a paper ball at another student and everyone started giggling. He made a second pitch and laughed out loud.

"Joseph Brisson, the door!"

"I'll take the door, if you can put me out," taunted Brisson.

This normally started a predictable sequence of events:
1. *The culprit leaves the classroom;*
2. *On patrol in the hall, Father Boutin would catch him;*
3. *Father Boutin would re-admit the student in class with the under standing that both the teacher and the student would meet with him at the end of the afternoon.*

But, in my mind, Brisson's defiant shout had altered the accepted routine.

I walked over in measured steps and lunged at him, throwing him violently against the wall. Then I swung him around and gave him the bum's rush out the door. The classroom was silent. I selected a poem and called for silent reading while I tried to simmer down.

Five minutes later, there was a knock at the door. I walked over, opened, and there was Father Boutin, with his habitual smile, ushering big Joe back into my classroom. I exploded. Joe was thrown out a second time; this time so violently that he hit the Director knocking him down. I closed the door and returned to my desk. Ages later, class ended.

"Father, I want to apologize for roughing you up this morning, it was an accident. Now, I'll tell you my side of the story."

An incident of this magnitude, concerning those pampered kids, called for a management meeting. The verdict was handed down late that evening. The administration had decided to stand by me.

"It's now up to you to decide: accept a clear and unequivocal apology from Joseph Brisson or expel him from the class, in which case he's expelled from the college," reported Father Boutin. "For the moment, Joe was told to stay home. At your convenience, we'll call him in and you will inform him of the decision."

The next day, I met with Brisson. He apologized very sincerely. I accepted and things got back to normal in my classroom. Not surprisingly, Joe and I became good friends. And I knew that I didn't want to spend my life teaching.

On March 21, 1938, Mom wrote that the family had a new addition, a ninth boy – Julien had come into our world. I prayed this was the happy ending we were hoping for because my mother was now 50 years old! Later, I was told that as soon as the baby was born, Dad picked him up and danced with him around the kitchen much to Antonio's amusement and to the dismay of little Julie who had lost her place as the center of attention. She didn't speak for a day or so.

A Master Carpenter
Ludger D'Amour

I was about seven years old when I first got to see a work of art in progress. Cyriac Gaudet, one of our neighbors, was busy making the baptismal font for our new church. It was a beautiful piece of furniture made from lowly birch flooring planks and using the most elementary rustic tools. It was to me at the time (and remains 80 years later) a fascinating work of art, a masterpiece of design and assembly. He was working at home, upstairs, his workbench made up of two 10-inch planks on two empty flour barrels. Fascinated, I watched his handiwork. It was like a revelation. I fell in love with woodworking and decided to make it my lifelong occupation.

My father was a handyman with wood and metal. He was a problem solver. But I don't think he ever had time to exercise his talent on fancy woodwork. In our workshed, there was a good variety of tools and that may explain how four of the nine boys in our family took more than a passing interest in carpentry.

From the time I was about six, I always managed to have a pocketknife of my own. Not always of the best quality, but adequate enough to sharpen a pencil, to change an empty thread spool into a spinning top and, in early spring, to transform a piece of alder branch into a whistle. From our toolshed, I would occasionally sneak away the spoke shave or the keyhole saw to work on some pet project.

These ventures in woodworking led to an early training in basic first aid to treat the cuts, nicks and bruises that I inflicted upon myself. Band-aids were not available at the time; so, for a cut, sucking blood was the recommended immediate action and a small cut would be covered with a little piece of newsprint. More serious cases called for a snug dressing made from an old and generally clean rag.

A few years later, Cyriac built our new home. I was waterboy. I watched carefully every phase of the construction. It was captivating to see how he made complex cuts and measurements, particularly for the dormer windows of the attic and for the stairway. There were no trade books or pocket calculators, no one could read the fineprint tables on the Sargeant steel square; but, somehow, he had a method to figure out the length and bevel cuts of the roof rafters, even the jack rafters had no secrets for him. Over the years, I watched him build stairways either straight, angled or with landings and each time the treads and risers were balanced to perfection.

Those mysteries were revealed to me years later at a trade school in Montreal by an instructor who did not possess half of Cyriac's practical knowledge.

Cyriac Gaudet had other talents. There was a lot of fighting going on in Baie-Ste-Anne. Yvon Durelle, the legendary Fighting Fisherman, was yet to be born but the fighting tradition was well established. There was even a Quarreling Hill.

Each small community had its champion who was called upon whenever outside bullies showed up. Cyriac was our worthy champion in Eel River Bridge. But he was also very kind both to his family and his community. He was a good father and a devoted husband. His volunteer work is legendary whether collecting for a worthy cause or making caskets as a service to the bereaved.

In 1935 I was hired as a carpenter helper in the repair and maintenance work on the W. S. Loggie fleet of 15 fishing schooners. Cyriac Gaudet was the foreman. At the time, some foremen barked and snarled at the workers, shouting and swearing, often in a foreign language to impress the men. Cyriac was like a good coach who spoke politely to every man. He was understanding and humane to beginners and unskilled workers. I was impressed with his intelligence, his skills in the many different trades involved in fishing-boat repairs, be it carpentry, scraping, oakum caulking or painting.

In the evening around the shanty stove, he would relate some of his experiences in problem solving, never bragging, just to impress on us not to give up when faced with a difficult task. He believed that there was always a way or two when common sense and sound judgment were used to the limit.

He showed me how to sharpen tools and, now that my hobby is woodcarving, I can assure you that nobody ever showed me a better technique. After more than 65 years, every time I sharpen tools for cabinet work, violin making and woodcarving, Cyriac's lessons come to mind.

On Loggie's fishing fleet, one of the 40-foot boats, *The Leader*, needed a new keel. The manager told us we could find a suitable tree on Loggie's Island. We crossed over early one morning only to discover that no tree on the island could provide us with a 40-foot keel, six inches wide and eight inches deep. Cyriac selected two yellow birches each a full 22 feet to the first limb. We cut them down. On site we trimmed and rough-hewed to make them lighter for transportation to shore, on our shoulders. They were tied behind the boat and towed to the mainland. It was a hard day's work.

We spent the next days planing, chiseling and trimming to assemble a first class keel. *The Leader* and her sister ships were in good repair in plenty of time for the launch that was carried out during the last high tide before June 1st. This undertaking showed well the foreman's leadership ability and personnel management techniques. The men respected his engineering, construction and woodworking skills and under his direction everyone gave his best effort. I never saw him lose his cool.

Each boat was launched by manpower. The carpenters, their helpers and the assigned boat crew gathered early one morning at the high ground area where the fleet spent the winter months. On her keel and flank, with pulpwood for rollers, each boat was pushed from the high ground to the shore and from the shore to the water. Everyone worked in good humor and diligently as the entire fleet had to be launched in a few hours - the tide did not wait. I never witnessed a single accident. For three consecutive seasons, I worked with him on boat repair.

After working six 10-hour days, living in a shanty with no comfort or services, late on Saturday afternoon he would walk home, a full seven miles with the family groceries on his back. Then on Sunday, he would walk to church and back, a nine-mile trek; and then, most Sunday afternoons, he offered barber service to whoever needed a good quality cut. He was also the master butcher for the village.

His generosity had no limit. He was never paid according to his talent or services. He often worked free of charge, sometimes exchanging services with a neighbour.

Cyriac Gaudet never owned a horse and wagon, he traveled on bicycle in the summer, on foot the other seasons.

He worked wonders with wood and quiet miracles with people. For me, he remains the Master Carpenter.

The Lumberjack

Ludger D'Amour

What was later labeled as the Great Depression was coming into its 6th year. It was January, 1936, and, as far as I was concerned, the economic wasteland was limitless; because, ever since I was old enough to look for work, there was none.

A provincial election was coming up. So, W.S. Anderson, Minister of Public Works, announced the construction of a highway that would cut the province of New Brunswick in half – 75 miles from Renous to Plaster Rock. Two jobs at $30 a month became available to the Baie-Ste-Anne area. Uncle Abdon, a lumberjack with 10 years experience was hired; I was elated to be told I had the other posting. I was inexperienced and a little apprehensive; my uncle was pessimistic, but work was work.

So as not to make our neighbors jealous, we left after dark. A friend accepted to drive us with horse and sled for a distance of eight miles. That left us with a 17-mile hike in the snow, carrying heavy haversacks and guided by the stars. It was viciously cold. We walked quickly to keep warm.

We got to Loggieville at four in the morning. Only the boiler room of the sawmill was open, the operator was on duty. For our breakfast, we waited next to the fire until the small hotel was open.

Soon we were on the train headed for Renous, we got there at 10. We were given directions to the job site and took off on foot for another 20 miles. Noon came and we were still passing farmhouses, a long way from the forest. We stopped at a few houses to ask for food and were turned down three times. At the fourth house, the dog welcomed us and the lady gave us some food. After this lunch we were told that we still had 10 miles to walk through the forest.

The cold persisted and I could feel blisters forming under the straps of my backpack. After a while, we caught up with four men. They were slowed down because one of them had hurt his foot and every now and then he had to remove his boot and walk in the snow in stocking feet. They were all about 40 years old. Misery had brought us together.

It was four o'clock when we got to the Colepaugh Camp and darkness was setting in. We were given a light lunch and some black tea. We still had five miles to go and it would be total darkness before we could get to the camp where we expected to spend the night.

We got to the first camp at six o'clock. We entered a shack where 40 men were already settled. A strong odor of leaf tobacco and dirty socks greeted us.

"Ludger, you picked a good time to become a lumberjack," said my uncle.

In 24 hours we had covered 37 miles on foot in difficult circumstances. The cook served supper. We were like soldiers of a defeated army. Someone handed us a few woolen blankets and we bedded on large crates with crosspieces strategically placed to make the night unbearable.

Next morning, it didn't take very long to wash up. We wolfed down breakfast and took off for a final four-hour trek. The blisters had burst and I could feel blood running under my haversack straps.

But the weather was clear and my companions, who had not said much the day before, made enthusiastic comments on the beauty surrounding us. The trees in this hardwood forest were some 60 feet tall with practically no branches except at the very top where the small crowns met to form a sort of canopy. Horse teams had carved trails between them. With the sunny sky and immaculate snow it could have been a walk in the park. It was like a Garden of Eden and I felt ashamed at the thought we would be cutting down these trees to build a highway.

At noon, we got to our camp. The cook served a good lunch, the camp was new and the men clean as they, like us, had just left home. We fixed our beds with spruce boughs and new blankets. Several work crews were formed and I ended up with one that spoke only English. They couldn't say "Ludger" – even though it's like "bluejay" without the "b" – so they called me Johnny. They were good people and, as I worked with them, I began to learn English.

After one month's work, we got our first paycheck, only 26 dollars! The veterans were disappointed, it was a new record low pay. They dispatched a letter signed by every employee asking the Minister of Public Works for a raise. Two weeks later, we got a positive response: one dollar a month! Our negotiators had neglected to specify the amount, trusting on the generosity of the Minister.

Life's lessons were coming at me hard and fast but it was almost unimportant. I had a job I liked, I was learning a trade, I didn't have any horses to care for,

I was in good health and I was well fed. All in all, I was a relatively happy young man.

The job lasted 70 days. March 15 was on a Saturday and because of heavy rain we were unable to work in the woods. Again the next day was very mild. Snow was melting and the streams were swelling fast. On Monday there was so much water running under the snow that we sank up to our waist with every step; even the deer had problems getting about. It was St. Patrick's Day, Spring was in the air and I was happy to be going back to my family. I had become a man.

We hitched a ride on a sled and our team of horses managed to cross the river in spite of the white waters and the increasingly powerful current. Once safely on the other side we watched, worried and fascinated, as a dozen horses with their Métis handlers crossed the raging torrent in a scene not unlike the most daring cowboy feats made in Hollywood.

Back to Renous, we went to Sullivan's Store while waiting for the train. A radio was playing Irish music – that was the first time that I heard a radio. We were back to civilization.

I had survived a rather good experience as a woodsman and I was confident that I was destined to a bright career as a first rate lumberjack.

I spent the winter of 1936-37 up the Cascapedia River, 44 miles north of Causapscal, Quebec. As happens in most other momentous events, if it was planned at all, it wasn't planned exactly the way it turned out.

I had gone to Newcastle looking for work and there was nothing available anywhere; so, I decided to check out the activities at the railway station. I was standing there admiring the giant locomotive when two young lumberjacks fully dressed for the part, complete with axe and crosscut saw on the shoulder, came on the platform to wait for the "All aboard". They were from Tracadie and told me there was work in Causapscal. I immediately got a one-way ticket and took the train for my first trip to Quebec.

After a few hours we got off at Causapscal. The train station was packed. The village had a county fair atmosphere with more than 400 unemployed already celebrating jobs that were yet to be. I was told the hotels and boardinghouses were booked solid.

Nonetheless, I decided to check out the Bellevue Hotel where, contrary to rumours, there were still a few places available. It was 50 cents for the night, not for a bed but just to get inside; there were no mattresses, pillows or blankets. I slept fully dressed, my haversack for a pillow and my wallet (with $12) inside my shirt. I was up early.

The employment office opened at eight o'clock but, before seven, a crowd of more than 300 men had already gathered there. On the balcony in front of the office, Lanky Lamarre, a sort of slave trader, began to pick out the men who appeared to be the strongest and toughest of the lot. I knew immediately, there would be no work available for the likes of me.

"Are you from the area?" asked a young man with the unmistakable accent of the Magdalen Islands.

"No, I'm from New Brunswick," I answered. "You sound like someone from the Islands," I added.

"You guessed right. What do you know about the Islands?"

"My parents and grandparents moved to New Brunswick from the Maggies about 25 years ago. And I know there are families of Turbides, Mom's relatives, who settled in Lac-au-Saumon not far from here. So, I guess I'll visit the relatives," I said with bravado.

"Can I come with you?"

Once again on foot, we headed out for Lac-au-Saumon. We climbed hills, walked down valleys, with this wearisome topography repeating itself over and over again. When we reached the village, we were told the Turbides were settled quite far in the backcountry. There were more hills and vales ahead of us, our packsacks were getting quite heavy and we were both hungry.

Finally, we got to the home of my great-uncle, Raphael Turbide, 75 years old. We were told we would find him "over there, at the far end of the field". It was harvest time and he was busy with his nephew, Prosper (60 years old) and two teenage girls, Alice and Germaine Chevarie. We learned later that all the other men were gone to the lumber camps.

The girls went back to the house and we were put to work. We loaded and unloaded several wagonloads of grain until darkness set in at about 10 o'clock. At last, we were invited to the house. I hadn't had a meal for the past 48 hours. The welcome was warm and the food delicious.

"We'll do the threshing tomorrow," said Uncle Raphael.

We helped with the harvest and the chores for five days. Meanwhile, they told us Léo, a second cousin of theirs, had obtained a lumber harvesting contract and they thought he didn't have all his crew. It was whispered that he was too demanding and the people who knew him would not work for him. I felt I was up to the challenge.

I was hired for $34 a month, shelter and meals included, and on October 14, at five in the morning, we were walking behind a wagon loaded with tools and other essentials. A team of tired horses led the way for a full 10 miles. Then we climbed in the back of trucks, packed like sardines and standing on beef carcasses that were served to us later on, in various forms of ragout.

At the 10-mile depot, we ate white vermicelli and white baking powder biscuits for lunch. I noted the cook's face was also uncommonly white. We were told we would be charged $2.50 for the meal and the transportation – I hadn't started working yet and I was already two days' work in debt.

We still had 14 miles to go and the road was impassable for the trucks; so, we walked the rest of the way. We staggered, slipped and foundered in the mud and over rocky terrain, often with water up to the knees. At 5 p.m., we reached camp.

It was a rundown shack and already 180 men were settled in. In some places icicles dangled over the bedding area. Someone pointed out the double bunks where there was still only one occupant. Now we had to wait for the men's return to find out whom we would bunk with – it was high drama.

They came in tired, dirty and unshaven. Some looked like murderers, all swore abundantly. It worried me that I was about to disturb one of these individuals who had had the advantage of a double bunk to himself for a couple of weeks. Finally, a fellow came and sat on the bunk I had selected.

"Can I bunk there?" I asked politely.

He grunted something that I translated into an enthusiastic "Yes". I discovered later that he was mentally challenged. Luckily for me, he didn't speak much because I could never make out what he was saying. Three weeks later, he left with his father because their horse was sick.

My next bunk companion was from Lac-au-Saumon, Omer Richard, a latecomer. We became good friends and talked together a lot. One night, we forgot ourselves after curfew and almost everyone threw a boot at us. I still wonder how they could aim so well in total darkness. We were reminded in no uncertain terms that there were no exceptions to the rule of total silence after the rosary and lights out.

Suppertime was uniquely impressive when 200 starving men set about to empty all the pots voraciously and in total silence. The atmosphere was intimidating, the décor dreary, the menu disgusting and many of the men scary. But I was determined to tough it out for at least three months.

Every day we walked three miles both ways in the dark. We might be slapped in the face by a branch, we could trip dangerously on a stump or stumble perilously in a hole. Safety was not an issue at work while survival was sometimes the issue on the way to and from the work site.

We were treated like slaves, whipped with cuss words. Legions of lice devoured us night and day. Sometimes we had to stop work and rub our backs against trees like animals.

Thank God for Sunday. We did the laundry and tried delousing one by one or by mass extermination in a tub of boiling water, when the tub was available. We refreshed the beds with new spruce boughs and, of course, wrote home or to the girlfriend. I also wrote letters for some of the other men – writing love letters was an interesting challenge. One of my friends received every week a six-page novella from his girlfriend, a schoolteacher. She never knew, I suppose, that he passed them around to some of us who enjoyed reading and writing as a leisure activity much preferable to playing cards or listening to the boring tales of old man Tremblay.

The Causapscal experience lasted four months and 10 days. An episode that had no redeeming features and that left me for a while with a low opinion of mankind in general.

In the fall of 1937, I decided to try again for a job in the lumber camps. I was staying in Scoudouc at the time, working as a farm hand for my uncle Arsène. In the immediate area, I didn't know of any company involved in cutting lumber. One day, Mr. Melanson, a door-to-door salesman told me about Pearl Beers Lumber in Sussex. I was 22 years old. Considering my experience, I figured I could earn as much as $40 a month this time around.

For today's reader, a few comparisons will illustrate a lumberjack's earning power: one day's work would earn you a pair of mitts; seven days, a pair of trousers; five days, a pair of shoes or a shirt. One hour's work would pay a pack of ZigZag tobacco, the cheapest, or three postage stamps. It took two hours to earn enough for a haircut; an average dress suit cost about four 60-hour weeks.

Working in the woods was exhausting physical work. Sunday was the only time off. Some of the men played cards or checkers; some exchanged tall tales and gossip; others wrote home or to the girlfriend. Like convicts waiting for the sentence to end, everyone's ambition was to tough it out until Spring.

Aldérice, a friend of mine, wanted to come along. It was his first season, so he was glad to join up with a veteran.

In early November, we left Moncton by train with one-way tickets. We got to Sussex at noon. We didn't waste any time looking for food, we asked a truck driver if he knew where Pearl Beers' camps were located.

"I'm going that way," he said. "I'll take you to about five miles from the camp."

The trucker had a helper, so we had to get in the back, on the platform. We sat on the spare tire, secured our packsacks, and grabbed hold of a chain. It was a bit cold, rain was threatening, the roads were in terrible condition but we were glad for the ride.

I didn't dare try to speak because the ups and downs, twists and turns would have caused me to bite my tongue off. After about 25 miles, we came to a truck that was stuck in a large mud hole and blocking the road. The driver and his sidekick had to help. We took off on foot for a distance of about 10 miles in unknown territory.

For hours we walked on muddy trails and the heavy cloud cover brought early darkness. Our eyes grew accustomed to the dark and, after some time, we could distinguish the dark form of trees against a lighter background. Freshly cut stumps stood out like beacons.

By this time, we figured we might have something like five more miles to go. The trail was getting more narrow and treacherous by the minute. I began to wonder how we could find a camp in total darkness, with so little information and without a lantern.

My companion was worried. So was I but I wouldn't admit it.

"Most camps are built close to rivers," I told him.

Every time we were going downhill, we listened anxiously for the sound of running water. Once, as we were going up a long incline, I suggested that it was our opportunity to smell smoke coming from the camp.

"On a damp night like this, I'm sure we can smell smoke for miles," I said to re-assure him.

I remembered one of my grandfather's many stories. This one was about a traveler lost in the woods. The poor man had walked, walked, walked and walked until he finally spotted a lantern light in the distance. When he got there, a witch was waiting for him with malicious intent. A light of any kind would have suited me just fine, and I wasn't afraid of witches.

Sometimes we would become aware of wild animals nearby. After more than an hour spent walking uphill and downhill, I think I had exhausted a full catalogue of positive suggestions.

Then we smelled something like smoke, it was urgent that we get the right drift from the whiff. We spotted a line of freshly cut stumps that we followed at a livelier pace; and, then, about half a mile away we could distinguish a weak reddish light. Then, a stronger smell of smoke. We had made it!

We headed straight toward the light. We crossed deep muddy puddles, staggered in the underbrush, tripped on stumps and fallen trees, and branches whipped us across the face. But our haversacks were lighter and we knew we'd find a place to spend the night; so, happy and relieved, we staggered on towards a human presence, a fire, a shelter and, maybe a bunk.

We reached the camp from the back. We sat on a pile of logs nearby to rest our weary legs and sore ankles. We hadn't spoken for more than an hour and lockjaw had set in from worry and fatigue. We were hungry and tired. But oh so happy! We looked at each other under the weak light from the camp and began to laugh. We laughed like fools, tears streaming. We couldn't stop.

We went in. It was Pearl Beers' camp.

A very hospitable man led us to the kitchen where his daughter served us leftovers from the supper, it was a banquet. We were assigned an upper double bunk, not too far from the stove. I have never felt better in my life – a 5-star hotel could never offer as much relief to a traveler.

We were taken on the payroll the next day. Everyone there spoke only English and I was able to improve on my rudimentary knowledge of the language. My friend, who spoke only French when we started work, became bilingual in the course of the winter.

As I look back, I suppose that Pearl Beers' Camp unknowingly offered two essential courses for the times: Orienteering 101 and English (total immersion).

So armed, I started on the road to higher learning.

A Secondary Education
Antonio D'Amour

It was a typical November evening with alter-
nating showers of wet snow and driving rain. We were
at the kitchen table playing cards while Mom was
writing a letter to one of her many relatives in fara-
way Iles-de-la-Madeleine, my parents' birthplace.

At his rolltop desk in the far corner of the living
room, Dad was in serious discussion with Colonel
Arthur Barry, regional superintendent of Fisheries for
northeast New Brunswick.

"Come over here Maurice, Mr. Barry wants to speak
to you," Dad said.

Maurice left the table and went over. Barry was
one of the bigshots who dropped in every now and
then to discuss important matters with my father.

"This morning as I was leaving the office, I was
informed that the delegate from Baie-Ste-Anne can't
make it to the training session in the co-operative
movement. This might be a great opportunity for a
young lad like you," said Colonel Barry.

Maurice looked at Dad.

"I agree with Colonel Barry, but it's for you to decide."

"What kind of training session is that?" Maurice inquired, thinking to himself Barry had made it sound like a military exercise.

"Actually, it's a university course. You'll have to go to Antigonish – that's in Nova Scotia – where you will learn about co-operatives and credit unions."

"When do I go?"

"You must be in Newcastle tomorrow. The train leaves at two o'clock."

That's how Maurice found himself at 17, with a grade six education, about to take courses in one of the most prestigious universities in Eastern Canada. It was 1936 and the Great Depression had already put us through seven years of disastrous economic drought.

Our village school normally offered classes up to grade seven, but in 1933-34 the school board had not been able to raise enough money to hire a teacher; so, we had stayed home that whole year. My father had subscriptions to a few newspapers; we were all avid readers and curious about the goings-on in the world. But more importantly, Cyrille and Roméo, my two older brothers, were in university and, whenever they came home with books, magazines and their vast vocabulary, the intellectual level of our conversations moved up several notches.

As Maurice considered his lack of formal education and his limited experiences, this venture looked to be the kind of challenge he had to accept. The next day, he was in Newcastle at Colonel Barry's office where Mr. Hédard Robichaud provided him with instructions, papers and train tickets.

At the train station he met two young men, a Robichaud from Shippagan and a McGraw from

Tracadie. All three were on their way to St. Francis Xavier University. The trip was going well and they had plenty to talk about. Near Truro the train seemed to shudder a bit and then stop. A wheel had jumped the track, they were told, and repairs would take four or five hours.

The trio got off the train in Antigonish very late that night. A cold wind whistled through the leafless trees. No one was there to meet them. They didn't know anyone and had no place to go.

"What do we do now? asked McGraw.

"I suggest we go to that hotel, over there," Maurice answered.

They slept well in the York Hotel that night, maybe too well. When they reported for registration they were told in no uncertain terms that they were 90 minutes late.

Maurice was billeted in a nice home. The owner was the local jeweler, a MacDonald. For 30 days they followed a strict regime of courses, lectures, conferences and the occasional field trip. He was impressed with the way the village of Pomquet had developed a successful Credit Union and a well managed Co-operative store.

Many notable gentlemen, including Angus L. MacDonald, Premier of Nova Scotia, came to speak to them of the importance of the co-operative movement and, in every address, they held out this formula as the pathway to economic nirvana.

There were about 50 students. Some came from Newfoundland, a few from Prince Edward Island, several from New Brunswick, and a large contingent from mainland Nova Scotia and Cape Breton Island. Although most of the discussions included anecdotes from the fisheries, many a Cape Bretoner had stories of hardship featuring the big mining companies.

The main instructor was Fr. MacPherson. Occasionally, Fr. Moses Coady would drop by but he was already very busy in his leadership role and he appeared to travel far and wide.

The program was designed to mirror the Rochdale movement originating from Great Britain. As had been the case in England, the large companies in our area kept our fishermen in virtual slavery by forcing them to work only to repay the previous year's purchases at the company store. If the co-operative movement were to liberate them, the trainees would follow its suggestions with enthusiasm.

On December 10, when Maurice returned to his boarding house, everyone was in an uproar. King Edward VIII had just announced his abdication. In August he had entertained the British Empire with stories of his pre-nuptial honeymoon sailing the Adriatic Sea aboard a chartered steam yacht with the American divorcee, Wallis Simpson. This time he was trading the British crown for Wallis' delights.

But royal escapades didn't influence the training syllabus. The trainees were motivated. The motivation came from the excellent quality of the curriculum offered by the university. It was re-enforced by a desire to work at improving the regional economy that still operated on a sort of feudal system.

And it wasn't all work. Occasionally, in the evening, Father McLaughlin would take out his fiddle and they had joyous dancing. For a young man from Baie-Ste-Anne, this was a totally new experience as dancing was considered a sin and the edict was underlined with threats of eternal damnation.

When Maurice got home from Antogonish, our parish priest, Father Gallien, asked him what he had learned at university.

"Father, I learned that your catalogue of sins can vary from region to region," he answered.

Nonetheless, that 30-day workshop had awakened in him a deep interest in business. Shortly after, he served the war years with the Canadian Army Pay Corps. Then he enrolled as a full-time student at the Success Business College in Moncton,.NB. This led to a good job in payroll and automotive parts in management for Price Bros., a major pulp and paper company in the Saguenay region of Quebec.

Years later, Maurice took over management of a large clothing store in Chicoutimi, a business which he later purchased and ran successfully for several years. At age 63, he moved to Quebec City in comfortable and secure retirement.

Today, as he looks back, he will tell you that his first step on the road from rags to riches was taken with the help of a 30-day co-operative training program at St. Francis Xavier University, in Antigonish, Nova Scotia.

The Universal Joint

Antonio D'Amour

My brother François (a.k.a. Frank) was the ninth of the family; eight before him and eight after him. Dad ran a general store near the bridge in Eel River Bridge. It was a wondrous place with every sort of food, clothing, automotive, fuel and hunting items. Two big front windows provided a good view of the road, the gas pump and the hitching post. Barns and warehouses held a multitude of other treasures to be discovered by a little boy.

We lived in a lovely home 100 feet from the store and close to the river just before it opened on the bay; a place of beauty in an age of innocence. When the kids played, there were lots of participants; there were people around to help, hinder, support or annoy each and every one of us everywhere and all the time. So, at an early age, each of us learned to cherish the occasional moments of solitude.

Frank loved to spend time upstairs in the general store when Dad, and occasionally Grandpa, served the customers. Marvelous inventions captivated his attention up there. He would spend hours trying all sorts of moves with a Ford Motor universal joint, a constant source of fascination; he also marveled at the complex, twisted links used to make up tire chains, so beautiful and so practical.

Store clerks had a lot to do because everything was delivered in bulk quantities, from candy to salt fish. No one had yet tried the smaller individual packaging formula except for some canned stuff. One day (late 1920s-early 1930s) the store got its first delivery of canned spaghetti – no one knew what spaghetti was. We took a can home and tried it, to everyone's surprise, it was good.

The family kitchen table was quite large with a sturdy five-foot bench against the wall and chairs to accommodate between 10 to 12 people for every meal. When guests and visitors showed up, there could be as many as 20 hungry mouths enjoying Mom's cooking.

Whether she was cooking, milking the cows or working in the garden, Mom sang all the time. She enjoyed old traditional songs and quickly learned the newest ditties from the gramophone. She never peeled less than a bucketful of potatoes and used up a new 100-pound bag of flour every week.

Grandpa loved to help with the wash. He enjoyed spending time pumping the long handle that activated the tub and conscientiously operating the wringer handle; he never ceased to marvel at this sophisticated technology.

Frank never liked vegetables. Dad and most of us (the boys) agreed with him; however, Mom, Grandpa and the reactionaries seemed to really enjoy veggies. To his dismay, Frank was often assigned gardening tasks and he never took a liking to them.

Whenever visitors would come, Frank and Dad would load their cars with all the turnips, beets and cabbages they could or would accept. How generous they were!

Time was tightly scheduled. We had schoolwork that was somewhat demanding as we were expected to merit good marks. The house chores revolved mostly around firewood and preparing food for certain animals. Barn chores do not need graphic description, either you know what's involved or you don't and, anyway, it has little bearing on your development as a Renaissance Man.

Sundays, religious feasts, first Fridays of every month and newly minted occasions called for church attendance. And that in turn required fasting – no food or water from midnight on. With an empty stomach, we would walk to church and back, a total of 10 miles.

Midnight Mass was a magnificent spectacle. From the time they got on the frozen bay, sleds loaded with the smaller kids and the grown-ups walking and running behind to keep warm, the magic of a special event was for all to see. Add to the scene a dozen horses, rows of clear bells jingling music with each step and the soft reddish light of the lanterns hanging from the front of the sled panels. Merrily, our eyes feasted on a vista of community celebration and religious fervour.

In return for our respect of the religious traditions and obligations of the day, we earned frozen ears, blistered feet and weariness in this life; we want to believe that we also amassed a rich trove of indulgences in the next.

In Frank's early teens he was introduced to the fishing industry, herring fishing in the early wet and cold Spring season. At five in the morning, Mom would prepare a generous breakfast of meat and potatoes that Ludger and he would wolf down before heading out to the river. Ludger would push out the heavy dory and

Frank would try out his muscles on the oars; they were headed for an area off Sandy Point, about three miles from home. Most days they could fill the dory to the gunwales with lively shining herring. Their next challenge was to row that load upstream and, more often than not, upwind. On their return, usually before noon, they would again eat like two hungry bears.

In the 1930's life was made up mostly of unrelenting and un-rewarded work, sandwiched between a set of stern religious rules and a warm friendly family atmosphere.

Then, Frank discovered pit props, a new backbreaking entry to the world of the lumberjack. At the time, it was the only possible source of employment.

When he was twelve years old, he began working on our grandfather's wood lot across the river from home. It was on a point of land that split the Eel River into north and south branches. To reach the job site, when he couldn't get the dory, he would walk up river and cross over the bridge, a one-mile trek.

Sometimes with an older brother, sometimes by himself, Frank cut pit props that, as the name suggests, were used by the mining industry. In winter, he cut pulpwood. Neither job generated any income to speak of, but it served well as basic training for further misery.

In 1938, he had the dubious privilege of becoming a professional lumberjack at age 15. He went to work about 125 miles from home, near Taymouth, an area 20 miles north of Fredericton. Other men from Baie-Ste-Anne were with him: Archie Schofield, George McIntyre, Émile Schofield and Nazaire Sippley.

They left home with no money, on foot and hoping the Good Lord would look favorably on hitchhikers. It was a long trip. More often than not, like his companions, his stomach ran on empty.

They started out cutting pulpwood and peeling the harvest with a shredder. The bark was removed easily as the wood was freshly cut but it was very slippery. Often, when they returned to cutting, they'd see the woodpile tumbling down a hill where they'd have to chase after the pieces and begin piling all over again.

On hot summer days, work sapped every ounce of energy. Salty sweat blinded them as they were harassed by thousands of flies with black bands on the wings, deer flies they were called, as they could pierce through thick deer hide; so human epidermis was no protection from their assaults. After a few days, Frank's neck and ears were eaten raw and bleeding. Infection set in with swelling and puss. It was an infernal torment with his ears stuck in the festering mass causing constant pain and leaving little opportunity to sleep.

The camp did not offer protection from invaders. Lice and other species of disease-carrying insects made everyone's life after work an on-going torture. Their plan called for a four-month stint and they were determined to tough it out. There was nothing else to do as Canada neared a full decade of the Great Depression. Occasionally he would think of his brother Roméo who, in spite of a university degree, had trouble finding a job. He would also call to mind Roméo's criticism of our economic and political systems.

"A clique of bastards have locked up the money vaults and are determined to bring everyone into slavery. Only the Germans got their economy going as it should," Roméo would say.

They returned home in the fall, in time for final harvest chores and preparing for winter woes with little money to show for their efforts.

The following year, they all re-lived the experience, another summer of torment.

This time, the new area, south of Taymouth, had little or no water; so, constant debilitating thirst was added to their nightmare. In the morning Frank carried about five gallons of water to the worksite and it was usually gone before noon. Then, as they were paid per cord of pulpwood one couldn't afford to wander about, water had to be found nearby. Best was a mud hole, a drinking hole for animals; or else a swamp where one would peel back the growth and scrape up the black water underneath – probably with deer shit and anything else Mother Nature added to her liqueur. They should have died from anything and everything but, somehow, they toiled on.

That fall, everyone registered for military service. Shortly after, Nazaire Sippley and George McIntyre decided to enlist. Enlisting meant going to Saint John, 120 miles away. They should have had to walk about 20 miles to the nearest bus or train station but, since they had no money, they knew that they were setting out on a 120-mile forced march. No money also meant no food. To survive, they helped themselves to turnips, potatoes and whatever else the farmers had left in the fields after harvest. Having enlisted in the Canadian army, the two fellows walked back to camp barefoot because their shoes had worn out long ago. Following this unheralded heroic act of citizenship, they resumed their job.

Most days seemed to be programmed with the same monotonous schedule of events. Sometimes a hardly funny incident was magnified into a hilarious joke just to make each one feel human again. Happily for them there were few accidents.

In an adjacent area, George McIntyre was busy cutting a tree into sections when Frank felt a sort of interruption. As he turned, he saw George fall down, holding on to his ankle. In seconds, the co-workers were with him. He had cut a deep gash in his foot.

Blood was spurting everywhere. They tried to close the cut and keep it shut as his foot was tied as snugly as possible to stop the hemorrhage. They then went to work making a stretcher of two burlap bags and two strong poles.

There was a 10-mile trail leading out to the road from where an ambulance could be called. It was a horrendous five-hour haul with four of the men carrying the load and two others to relay the most tired of the stretcher-bearers. George moaned every now and then but he bore the pain with incredible stoicism.

He was in the hospital and convalescing for a long time.

Frank left with Archie and Émile early one October morning. Loaded down with packsack, bucksaw and axe, they walked from the camp near Taymouth to McGivney, a long tiring walk. They got there shortly after two o'clock in the afternoon. Frank wasn't sure he wanted to go any further that day. They paused to admire a car parked near the general store. A man came out of the store and went to the new automobile, opened the door and, as he was to get in, he spotted the three lumberjacks.

He went to the back of the car, twisted a handle and opened the rumble seat.

"Get in boys," he said.

They managed to fit themselves in with their gear and off they went on a wonderful drive to Boiestown, 35 miles closer to home. The Good Samaritan was the local doctor, a wonderful man who also happened to own the Boiestown drugstore. Frank will be eternally grateful for his kindness and generosity.

The season was over and it was to be his last experience as a lumberjack, the end of his journey in hell. And with World War II moving into high gear, new and very different experiences awaited François.

Maurice Gets A Car

Antonio D'Amour

As usual, Cyrille, my elder brother, got the ball rolling.

"Maurice, a car would be very useful to the family and to the neighbours," he said. "Should you decide to get one, I'll contribute $50."

That's how, on August 14, 1937, Maurice found himself buying his first car at Lounsbury's garage in Chatham, New Brunswick.

He had learned the theory of driving but hadn't had any practice and he had no driver's permit, so Mr. W. P. Stackhouse, the manager, sent one of his clerks. The road check was superficial; they went a few miles along the Chatham Head Road.

Registration cost $2.00 and gas was 50 cents per gallon. He paid the $250 and became the proud owner of one of the classic vehicles of the era. It was a stately fence-post green, 1929 Nash with 65,000 miles of cruising the horrific roads of the time.

Luckily, Maurice spotted Mark MacDonald, an acquaintance; he knew Mark had a driver's permit. Mark agreed to be Maurice's driver from Chatham to his house in Hardwicke (about 20 miles). With about 10 miles to his home in Eel River Bridge, Maurice bravely took his first solo. By the time he drove in the yard, half an hour later, he felt like a seasoned chauffeur.

The entire neighbourhood gathered around the Nash. The women were impressed with the fancy tasseled curtains and the greenish gray plush interior. Every man took on airs, asking questions that would show off his knowledge of automotive technology and which, every time, highlighted Maurice's limits in that field. Finally, that ordeal over, Mom served her usual hearty and tasty meal and, exhausted, he fell into a deep sleep with dreams of herding an unending line of Nash cars.

The next day was Sunday. Maurice didn't feel he should run the risk of driving the whole family to church, so he got our neighbour, Bertie Jenkins, to take his place; the Nash carried a full load. For a few days he practiced driving around the village where traffic was limited and cops forever absent. Then he tried his first trip to Chatham and went for his driver's test that was carried out by one of Dad's many friends. He passed with flying colors. Now the highways and byways were his to explore.

On his next trip to Chatham, he had a full load of passengers; they split the $5 fare among all six or seven of them. Maurice had traveled that road many times with horse and buggy or sleigh. He believed he knew most of the people along that 30-mile route. Most, if not all, were always happy to offer assistance and shelter in difficult times. But travelling in his Nash he enjoyed protection from the elements and good speed in spite of terrible road conditions.

The short stretch of pave between Loggieville and

Chatham (less than five miles) provided the only moment when he could break the 20 mph barrier. The Nash offered a few puzzles and some mysteries. The gas tank was in the rear, as in most of today's vehicles but there was no gas pump. The wipers operated through a vacuum system, he was told, but they would not budge when going uphill. The two front tires were 550/19 (both Firestone), the rear tires (one was a Bulldog from Eaton's, the other a Dominion) were 600/19. A flat tire was a catastrophe because the spokes were made of wood with a steel rim to support the tube and the tire. It required great care to replace a tube over the steel rim and not cut the valve off in the process, due to a spring operated mechanism that tightened the rim around the spokes. The front brakes were covered and somewhat reliable; the rear brake drums were uncovered, so he had no rear brakes when he passed all those muddy patches of road.

Maurice owned the only passenger car in the community. He drove several times to Chatham to pick up relatives or friends of the family and neighbors who came to visit us. For example, when Emilienne, Cyriac Gaudet's sister, came to Baie-Ste-Anne with her husband on their honeymoon, he drove with Cyriac to pick them up in Chatham; he was the designated chauffeur for Alphée and Philomène Mazerolle's wedding; and, on a more sombre occasion, he took Joe and Suzanne Martin to their son Clifford's funeral.

Early in December, my brother Cyrille who was curate in Atholville at the time, came down for a visit. Maurice was supposed to pick him up in Loggieville where the CNR railway spur from Newcastle ended. The morning he was to leave, a snowstorm forced his Nash to seasonal confinement. The other option was Barney, our horse.

My father always treated animals, especially horses, with great respect. He was concerned about this journey as Barney had not had any long trips since August 14, the day Maurice had bought the car. Dad laid out carefully the driving sequence to compensate for Barney's lack of conditioning: where to walk the animal and where to trot him. With our beautiful black sleigh, Barney and Maurice covered the 30 miles in five hours. They picked up Cyrille and returned home in less that four and a half hours, as a horse always travels faster when heading home.

Winter went on forever. Finally, after nine trips to Chatham with Barney, Maurice was ready to put the Nash back on the road.

For a little more than a year he enjoyed that car but made regular visits to the car lot in Chatham where newer and more practical vehicles were offered. A blue panel truck caught his eye. He thought he could make a bit more money carrying merchandise as well as passengers with this vehicle. Maurice traded in his Nash and filled out the papers for the less glamorous Chevrolet panel truck.

As he was about to leave Lounsbury's, Les Kirkpatrick, the sales manager, came to him.

"How old are you, Maurice?"

"Nineteen."

"That means you've been driving for over a year and your father never signed for you. You have to be 21 to own a car."

"So, what can we do about that today?" asked Maurice.

"Go home. I'll get your father's signature next time I'm in Baie-Ste-Anne."

Maurice reported that conversation to my father who told him he would gladly sign for the vehicle.

"I know I can trust you to respect the terms of your contract with the bank; but I can only trust you completely if you stay away from liquor. Should you start drinking, we'll re-evaluate the situation," said my father.

Dad would enjoy the occasional drink, once or twice a year, but only small amounts and in good company. To this day, Maurice doesn't touch alcohol.

In 1938, Dysart had been Premier of New Brunswick for three years. He had campaigned with the slogan "Good Roads Dysart". Although some efforts were made to improve road conditions generally, our area would not benefit from such lofty ambitions. For many more years our roads were practically impassable with large muddy ponds and crevices that tested the ability and resourcefulness of every car and truck driver.

Maurice installed two long wooden benches on each side of the panel truck to take several passengers to church every Sunday. Always with a full load and with a heady mix of perfume, pipe tobacco and barn aromas, the more than five-mile trip from home to church was carried out in relative comfort.

With the panel truck, Maurice found more work. Several times he drove 80 miles to Richibouctou on business. The roads were so bad where Dysart's contractors were at work that vehicles had to stop until a tractor would tie a towrope and haul them through oceans of mud to somewhat firmer grounds.

Two or three times that year, he went to Scoudouc, at Uncle Arsène's place to see my brother Ludger. On one trip my sister Geneviève and her husband Nelson Schofield came with him. In Shediac, 135 miles from home, he bought barrels of apples.

There was a restaurant in Eaton's store in Moncton (140 miles away) where he managed to sell several loads of oysters and lobsters. It wasn't easy work for him, Maurice weighed about 110 pounds and oyster barrels weighed twice as much. The loading platform at Eaton's was more than six inches higher than the floor of his panel truck, unloading was often a Herculean task.

In 1940, he sold his truck and left to find work in the Saguenay region, north of Quebec City. His career in transportation was over. But, somewhere in the back of his mind, he still savours the glorious times when he would crisscross the Miramichi area in a stately 1929 Nash.

Inspector of Fisheries
Roméo D'Amour

Lady Luck (or my Guardian Angel) once again came to my rescue. I would have work this winter. The Inspector of Fisheries had resigned because of age; he was also very sick. It was a political appointment. My father went to work for me and it paid off. I got the job of Temporary Inspector at a salary of $150.00 per month. I had never had so much money. Finally, I could begin to pay back my father for all the things he had done for me.

I was briefed by Chief Inspector Colonel Barry, my boss; sworn in, given the book on Rules and Regulations, handed my badge and my inspector's stamp. Now, it was up to me.

Will Savoie was my assistant; Will was an experienced and reliable man. Two other men were assigned to help us on the boat. We had about 30 miles of coast to cover. The first weeks on the job dealt with oyster fishing.

A license for oyster fishing cost 50 cents. Anyone with a rowboat and a rake was considered outfitted. The fishermen only got $1.00 per barrel, and that was for a full day's backbreaking work. Size limits were three inches for cup oysters and four inches for the thin-lipped. When fishing started not one license had been purchased.

My father was very much aware of the fishermen's plight. He suggested that I allow the poor fellows two weeks to get their 50 cents for the license. It looked humane and logical to me.

On my second day on the job, we went patrolling off Hardwicke. I spotted a group of about 30 rowboats and asked the patrol boat captain to turn on the speed. A dozen fishermen escaped by rowing furiously towards the shore. The others waited in resignation.

"I haven't got 50 cents," said one.

"That goes for me... and for me... and for me, too," joined the others.

"No problem today, my friends," I said. "Come to the patrol boat and get your license and sign my book."

They came over and the business was handled as well as could be expected. Everyone was relieved that there had been no need for confrontation.

"Now, fellows, you owe me 50 cents. Tell the guys on the shore that I offer them the same deal. And I'll be back in two weeks to collect."

Undersized oysters remained as the major problem. Spot checks could not keep everyone honest and it was an impossible task to check each and every rowboat.

Near Fox Island, there was a large oyster bed called by the locals *"La-quoi-qu'cé-ça"*, it had been declared out-of-bounds because it had been raked unmercifully and only baby oysters remained. Every time we passed the area, we could see rowboats there. We were easily spotted from afar and the fishermen had ample time to hide in the tall grass and the sand dunes of the island. So, we decided that the only way to get a handle on this was to hit the oyster packers, the markets themselves.

We started with a visit to an oyster packing house in Bay-du-Vin. As we got there, a big truck was loading up. Every barrel head carried the No.1 stamp of approval in big red letters – No.1 was my stamp! I called the packer.

"Good morning, Ernie,"

"Good morning," he answered. "Lovely day isn't it?"

"Where's this truck going?"

"It's just about ready to leave for Newcastle."

"Were the oysters inspected?"

"Don't worry, Roméo, they're all stamped."

"Yes. I see that… with my stamp. I want the barrels off the truck, opened and dumped for inspection. I don't care if it takes all day."

"Look, this truck is late already. I can't start unloading now!"

"If this truck moves, it'll be intercepted by the RCMP on the highway. It will go to Newcastle when I say so."

There was a chorus of curses as the nail pullers went to work releasing the barrel tops. Will Savoie carried out the inspection and I went with Ernie to his office.

"Now, Ernie, bring me all the stamped barrel heads that you have in stock. And I suppose you'll know what to do with them."

Two of Ernie's men got busy with the planer all the while wishing out loud that someone would do everybody a favor and shoot me on the spot.

I didn't press the issue but I made a detailed report to Colonel Barry who seemed pleased to see that something was being done to protect the many oyster beds in risk of total depletion by over-fishing.

I discussed this incident with my father. He liked to keep tabs on my activities and he tried to help in every way he could. He often cautioned me not to be over-zealous and to keep my temper in check.

"You have to reconcile two different and almost opposing principles," he once said. "On one hand, the observance of the law is very important; on the other hand, you must earn the respect and the friendship of the fishermen."

Smelt fishing began on December 1. There were no takers for the $1.00 fishing license; so, once again, I sold the licenses on credit.

The fishing technique involved a box net and a leader. A full net could yield as much as 1000 pounds of smelt. The harvesting process involved closing the mouth of the net, securing the lower lip on the ice and pulling the top part until the catch was spilled on the ice. On hitting the ice, the smelt would freeze up and the catch was preserved for delivery to the buyers.

The main regulations stated that you were forbidden to block the channel, a set distance had to be maintained between nets and the length of the leader could not be more than 90 feet. The first leader that I checked measured 130 feet. I advised the fishermen that I would grant a three-week delay to bring their oversize leaders within legal limits.

The fishermen objected strongly.

"We've been fishing with 130-foot leaders for years," argued one.

"How can you pull out a leader and set it back under very thick ice?" asked another.

"You could start with your uncles Alphonse, Gérard and Pierrot, and see if you can get them to budge."

I went to see Uncle Al at once. He was smiling.

"Of course they told you to come and check my leaders; don't bother, they're all oversize. I'll agree to the regulation if you can get everyone else to do the same."

By December 15, all leaders were within the allocated limit. I had had to chop off a few nets to get the message fully across but, from then on, the rules and regulations were respected and my job became a lot easier.

With horse and sled, I patrolled the smelt fishing area. On that immense field of ice, there were about 60 shanties that provided shelter to the fishermen when the sub-zero temperature got impossible. Most shanties offered hospitality, heat, friendship, coffee and (you guessed it) fried smelt.

About 150 fishermen in my area were getting ready for May 1. They had been hard at work since early March.

On April 29, a bright and sunny morning, my brother Maurice drove Will Savoie and I to check on the Baie-Ste-Anne fishing fleet. All 44 boats were anchored to the ice. I could see some activity on six of them but I knew every crew was chomping at the bit in anticipation of the word GO that was to come at 6 a.m. the following Monday morning.

Then Maurice drove us to the Escuminac breakwater. All week the roads had been practically impassable, it took longer than usual to get there.

As we neared the place I could see 31 boats at anchor, loaded and ready to go. Then I saw six boats leaving the bay. They were heading out to sea at full throttle. Some fishermen spotted me and came on the run.

"Roméo, those bastards are heading for the lobster grounds and the best spots. That's not fair!" they said.

I watched them go, disappointed. I wondered why they had chosen to shatter the serenity of this sunny day. I reflected that those 12 men were thumbing their noses at 138 of their friends and neighbors.

"They won't get away with it," I promised.

"What can you do about it? Your patrol boat is locked in the ice two miles up the bay," one answered back.

There was a lot of grumbling.

"Some of us will have guns on the boats and, because they have chosen the best spots, they'll think it right to chop our lines if we cross theirs. That's when the guns will come out."

I returned home to discuss the situation with Dad and my brother Maurice. We came up with a plan. At 2 a.m., Maurice and I left home, picked up Will and in less than an hour we were near the lobster cannery. The boats were out there close to one another, a good 100 feet of loose ice from the shore. Near the boats, I guessed the water would be about 6 to 10 feet deep.

About 60 fishermen, already at the cannery, had spotted us and were fighting mad.

"Where were you yesterday?"

"You're too late. You can't do anything now."

As planned, Will and I started cautiously from ice floe to ice floe to reach the fleet. We didn't get much support from the fishermen and, as we got about half way to the fleet, I heard one of them saying:

"I hope the bastards drown!"

It was a dangerous journey from the shore to the boats but we got there okay. We found what we expected to find. Most of the boats carried a full load of fishing gear; six of them were empty, thus pleading guilty. It took us about an hour to check the names and registration numbers.

When we looked over the side of the last boat, we realized that we were trapped. The rain had softened the ice to mush. I looked for a more consistent chunk of ice and found one close to the stern. I checked my jacket and tightened my belt. Gingerly, I stepped on the ice while holding on to the boat.

"Stay put, Will. I don't know how I'll do this but I'm going to try."

My first move went well but the ice floe was rather small and unsteady; so, when I spotted a larger floe coming my way, I immediately jumped. To my surprise it had the consistency of whipped cream. Down I went in the icy water and, to my astonishment, I shot right up. For brief moments my clothes would keep me afloat. I began to swim in the direction of another floe, reached it and tried to climb up, but it broke in two and down I went again. There was another larger chunk close by so I swam to it, dragged myself partly up and rolled over. As I looked up, I saw Will about to try something desperate.

"Don't move, Will. I'm okay here for now."

Instantly, the fishermen had started a rescue operation.

"Stay where you are. Don't try to get up. We're coming for you," someone shouted. And it struck me that it was the same voice that had shouted earlier:

"I hope the bastards drown!"

I stayed on my back, rolled down the top of my hipboots and lifted my legs to let some of the water out. Out of the corner of my eye, I could see four men coming towards me with long poles and a rope. It took about 20 minutes to get me to shore. On the boat, a much happier Will was still waiting for his rescue.

The fishermen gathered around me.

"Did you get all the names?"

"I got them all."

The shouts and applause had the spontaneity of a standing ovation. But I had to move fast, I was freezing. A group of men managed to get Will to shore while they took me to Abe's house. Abe owned the cannery and most of the fleet out there. As soon as I got in the house, I took off my boots, removed my jacket and checked my wet notebook. The penciled entries were legible and I left it open to dry.

Abe brought me some dry clothes. He refused any money.

"Roméo, I'm happy a tragedy was averted," he said.

After I had changed my clothes and had a few minutes to warm up by the stove, Abe came back.

"Tell me," he asked. "Did you manage to identify the boats?"

"Here are the names and registration numbers," I said as I showed him my notebook. He came over to read the list.

"You have two of mine and four of Loggie's. Mine, I don't care, they went without my permission but I'll pay the fine, anyway. But to think you have four of Loggie's, I could cry for joy. Nobody, but nobody, has ever dared to put a Loggie's boat under seizure. Four!..."

I rushed back to the edge of the breakwater. It was almost six o'clock. I raised my arm and, at six exactly, my arm came down and I shouted:

"Good luck!"

Unleashed, the entire fishing fleet roared out to sea. The sun was coming up with the subtle hues of late dawn. It was a most impressive sight, a fisherman's tableau of the on-going quest for a better quality of life.

Maurice came back to pick me up and we made a brief stop at home. Before eight o'clock, I was at Colonel Barry's office. Barry, a World War One veteran, ran his department as he had his regiment. He was fussy on appearance.

"You can't look a man straight in the eye and give him hell if you're in need of a shave and dressed like a bum," was his motto.

He enjoyed the report and, after a few minutes, he called in his boss, Mr. Sutherland to "come and hear this".

I recommended that no confiscation of gear or boat be made and there should be no fines; however, the guilty parties would go out, fetch their ropes, spars, anchors and buoys. At the wharf, the gear would then be inspected. I suggested that the penalty was stiff enough as they would lose five fishing days and the best lobster fishing spots.

But I was nearing the end of my nine months as Temporary Fisheries Officer. Again, I had to look for work and, this time it seemed harder to take. Colonel Barry was genuinely sad to see me go and he assured me that he would try to line something up for me in the Department of Fisheries.

Maurice was very disappointed as we had enjoyed a few interesting adventures together. My father, who had provided me with his enlightened support, felt a strong sense of loss at the thought that I would have to go elsewhere for work; but because of this short time we had spent together, I felt that I had become a better man.

The Salt Fish Board

Roméo D'Amour

In July, Colonel Barry called. There was a possible job offer in Halifax.

"You're on stand by," he said. "I'll call in a few days."

Three days later, he called again.

"Be at my office by eleven o'clock tomorrow morning. You're on your way to Halifax. The Salt Fish Board has just been formed and they're looking for an executive secretary; that's where you come in."

It was about two months before war was declared. There were hundreds of applicants for every job available. Once again, it looked like Colonel Barry was playing Guardian Angel for me.

In Newcastle, a Mr. McInnerny from Halifax was going back to his office and he was to take me with him. We reached the city early that evening and Mr. McInnerny invited me to stay at his home. After supper, he called the President of the Salt Fish Board, Dr. D. B. Finn and after a lengthy conversation he came to me, a worried look on his face.

"What, exactly, did Colonel Barry tell you about this job?" he enquired.

"He told me the job was mine," I answered.

"As you know, I just spoke to Dr. Finn and, according to him, he never told Colonel Barry you were hired. As a matter of fact, he has someone else in mind for the job."

I was speechless.

"Here's what I suggest you do. On my way to the office tomorrow morning, I'll drop you at the door of the Salt Fish Board. Be alert and, as soon as Dr. Finn comes in, follow him to his office. Don't let anyone get ahead of you."

At 10:30 I had the job and I was given an office. I was now Secretary of the Salt Fish Board but I believe that I was still in shock. I gave thanks to God and to my Guardian Angel.

Most of my first day was spent looking over a mass of applications for the position of steno-typist. It was urgent to fill this position as a lot of correspondence was already waiting. Later that afternoon, in walks a bright young man, just out of school, with a strong letter of recommendation addressed to Dr. Finn and signed by Énoïl Michaud, Minister of Fisheries. Naturally, Mr. Sirois was hired on the spot.

The Salt Fish Board was a creation of the Federal Government. It was set up to open new markets for Canadian salt fish in the Caribbean and in the USA. Norway was one of our competitors but the big competition came from Newfoundland, still a British colony at the time. The Salt Fish Board was run by its President, Dr. D. B. Finn and a Board of Directors made up of: Bert McInnerny, Chairman of United Maritime Fishermen; Professor Stuart Bates, Economist from Dalhousie University; Captain

William Deal from Lunenburg and others of equal standing.

Dr. Finn was an Englishman with a very special accent. At times he would leave me wondering "What the heck did he say?" Bill Sirois, the steno-typist, was a bit shy and, on the very first day, he was called to the President's office. Dr. Finn wanted to dictate four letters. Bill came back to my office with his stenobook and a worried look on his face.

"I'm puzzled by one of the letters Dr. Finn gave me."

"What's the problem?" I asked.

"It begins with 'Dear Cenotaph'. I know it can't be right but that's the way it sounds to me."

"Did you ask him to repeat?"

"I did and he repeated but that didn't help any."

Immediately I went to Dr. Finn and told him about Bill's problem.

"Problems with my accent," he said with a chuckle.

He pulled out the long list of members of the Salt Fish Board and pointed to the name of Senator Duff. That cleared it. Bill typed the four letters and brought them to me. They were very well typed; the margins well-balanced, no mistakes, no erasure marks; they were fit to be photographed as model letters. I brought them to Dr. Finn who was delighted.

"Now, Dr. Finn, Bill is still upset about his failure to understand your salutation to Senator Duff. Could you please take a minute to re-assure him because I think we have the best steno-typist in the Department of Fisheries."

"I'll do it with pleasure and right now!"

Bill got a near apology from the boss for his "most awful British accent".

"And, Bill, if you don't get it the second time ask me to spell it out," said Dr. Finn obviously enjoying himself.

The next day we had our first full meeting of the board. I immediately understood that preliminary meetings had already been held and a plan of action was in place. The meeting was to spell out clearly, polish and approve the wording of the Board's recommendations to the government officials.

It had been decided some months previously that the best way to fight the price war with our competitors was to subsidize the export of fish. Some $250,000 had been earmarked by the Department for that purpose and the Board had been created to find ways and means of providing subsidies while at the same time avoiding counter-veiling duties which the importing countries were bound to apply against Canada.

The idea was to subsidize the fishermen directly via a mind-boggling scheme. The merchants had to provide the fishermen, at time of purchase, with a receipt detailing the number of pounds of fish: cod, mackerel, herring, hake or halibut in one of the following stages of preparation: green, gutted, wet-salted or dry-salted. The Board would then apply the proper subsidy rate for each kind of fish in the state of preparation indicated at the time of sale. A subsidy form was then sent to Ottawa and a check was issued directly to the fisherman.

"Baffle'em" was the name of the game. The plan was successful and the salt fish started moving out.

Then war broke out. For some months the Board attended to its business as usual; however, we all knew that soon we would be asked to close the shop. Norway was now out of the competition; Newfoundland and Canada were allies. The great wheels of industry began to turn, markets opened up and the men were trooping to the colours.

In late July 1940, I joined the Naval Reserve. The course offered was meant to qualify me as a naval officer. I was still on the payroll at the Board where activity was down to a crawl.

War Years
Roméo D'Amour

The German armies had raced through Belgium. France had surrendered. The allies were playing catch up with the war effort and hoping for brighter days. General de Gaulle was somewhere in England trying to organize a semblance of French Resistance. And, in Halifax, a number of ships from the French fleet were in the harbour.

Naturally, I sought the company of Frenchmen brought to the city by the fortunes of war. A few short weeks earlier, I had seen the French aircraft carrier *Jeanne d'Arc*. It was on its way to the USA to pick up a load of planes that had been bought by the French government – eventually the ship docked in Guadeloupe where it remained for the rest of the war, its planes rotting.

Previously, I had visited the mighty battleship *Dunkerque* with its clusters of 40-centimeter guns. I met several of the sailors at a bar and got to know a few of them. Their new and varied accents, true melodies of our common language, were music to my ear. I was appalled when I learned that the *Dunkerque* had been scuttled in the port of Toulon.

And here, the luxury French liner *France* had been herded up the harbour by the British Navy immediately following the fall of France.

Ships of all designs and sizes sailed to and from Halifax. I loved that city. From my office window, I could see destroyers, submarines and merchant ships in constant traffic patterns and complex maritime maneuvers.

Every night was total blackout, all over the city. Whenever planes were heard, searchlights would poke long luminous fingers in the sky. The locals feared a repeat of the 1917 disaster when a ship had exploded and devastated Halifax. One night there was near panic; we awakened to the sound of cannon fire that went on for 10 long minutes. We were informed later that a merchant ship with ammunition on board in the center hold had caught fire. The navy had ordered a destroyer to sink the vessel and, with its hull full of holes, the ship went down. Halifax had experienced a near miss.

Our steno-typist, Bill Sirois, resigned from the Board and joined the Navy. A friend of mine, Raymond Delaney from the Islands, had been studying as wireless operator; upon graduation he joined the Navy also. Bill Sirois was soon appointed secretary to the Vice-Admiral in charge of setting convoys bound for England. He was one of the few men who had advanced knowledge of the Top Secret instructions prepared for the convoy commanders – these instructions were sealed and not to be opened until the ships were well out at sea.

Raymond Delaney was about to board the former *SS Prince Rupert* that was being outfitted as a raider.

And, a few months later, he returned to Halifax from a stint in the Caribbean. He was about to undertake a long sea voyage through the Panama Canal and down the Pacific Coast of North America in an effort to intercept German merchant vessels trying to sneak out of Peruvian ports. On that assignment, the *SS Prince Rupert* was to become quite successful. But the captured German crews could only be landed in Canada and that meant a long trip for the raider right up to Vancouver each time she filled her quota.

In mid-October, I received a letter from the Navy. I was to report for active duty in late November. I left my job at the Salt Fish Board and reported to Halifax for military service on November 26.

Each morning, for three consecutive days I reported to the Naval Barracks. Each time I was told to wait for my name to be called. For endless hours I sat in a waiting room reading and chain-smoking. On the morning of the fourth day, I was in the mood to start my own war.

I was getting the run-around and I couldn't find out what the problem was. Finally, a recruiting officer told me I was the problem because the regulations had been changed and no one could enlist in the Navy as an officer – my Probationary Sub-Lieutenant registration card was meaningless.

"You have to enlist as a seaman," he said.

"I'm already enlisted as an officer candidate. I won't sign up for anything else."

"You don't have any choice in the matter."

"My choice is to walk out of here and you know where to stuff those damn papers," I answered angrily and walked out.

Two days later I was in the Maggies where I spent the Christmas holidays.

In early January, I received my draft papers from the Army. I wrote back that I was the holder of a Navy registration card and I gave them my serial number. That seemed to put an end to the Army's claim on me.

I decided to try my luck with the Air Force. I reported to a Royal Canadian Air Force recruiting office and, after a medical check-up and a series of aptitude tests, I met the recruiting officer.

"I want to train to be a fighter pilot," I said.

"Sure. Everyone wants to be a fighter pilot. We need gunners and navigators also. Anyway, you're too old to be a pilot."

He was right. At 27 I was considered too old. So, I decided to try the Army once again. This time I reported to Fredericton, New Brunswick. I underwent another medical and the same series of aptitude tests. The basic training lasted a full week but we were not provided with uniforms, most of the men ruined their clothes and ended up without shoes.

One of the officers was honestly trying to help.

"I suggest you sign up for the Medical corps."

"I'm not a doctor, I'm not a nurse and I'm not interested."

"How about the Armored Corps... Tanks, you know."

"Thanks but no tanks. I want to be a foot soldier. What's the matter, has the infantry gone out of style?"

"With your college education, I'm sure we can find something better than that. And there's also your medical."

"What about my medical."

"Your feet are a mess, you'll never be accepted in the infantry."

"I'm leaving. I'm going home."

"You can't do that."

"Watch me."

I went back to the barracks to pack up and, the next day, I was back in Baie-Ste-Anne. With my useless Navy registration card, I was barred from seeking a civilian job. I argued the point with several specialists in bureaucratic ineptitude and, three months later I received my civilian registration papers.

Once again, I was broke, unemployed and, any day, subject to a second draft notice.

The Saguenay
Antonio D'Amour

It was early summer 1940. One year earlier, Adolf Hitler had launched his devastating military and propaganda offensive on Germany's immediate neighbours. Western civilization was reeling from the onslaught.

In North America, our economic and political gurus, who had kept the population in abject misery for a decade and more, found ways to crank up the economy. At the time, it seemed ironic that it had taken the enslavement of many European nations to liberate millions of North Americans from the sufferings imposed by a handful of moneylenders and their political accomplices.

But here, in Baie-Ste-Anne, there was pressing business at hand. Eugène Richard, Antoine Thériault and my brother Maurice were busy digging a grave in the village cemetery. Uncle Nectaire had died.

Uncle Nectaire was a very close friend of my father. He was well read and enjoyed spending hours discussing current events where politics was his forte. He was a respected elder. He had been with the early waves of settlers who had left Les Îles-de-la-Madeleine for Baie-Ste-Anne, New Brunswick. In earlier days, he had sailed the Atlantic seaboard with Louis-Léopold D'Amour and Martin Turbide, my grandfathers.

The entire community would be present the next day to pay respects and show affection. The three young men felt honored to play their part in this ritual.

"When do you plan to leave for the Saguenay region?" asked Antoine.

"Very early in August," Eugène answered. "We want to be there before school opens."

"The sooner, the better," Maurice added. "They say there will be more work in early September and I don't want to miss out on that."

With a couple of powerful strikes of his pick, Antoine smashed a few more layers of porous rock. Swiftly, like a gymnast, he bounced out of the hole. Maurice replaced him and started scraping the bottom.

"At least you'll be able to tell the guys in Quebec that you qualify as gravediggers," said Antoine as he reached down to grab the shovel handle and easily pull his friend out of the pit.

A few weeks later, they took the train for Rivière-du-Loup, the ferry across the St. Lawrence River to Saint-Siméon and a taxi for Kénogami where the Price Brothers Company Limited pulp mill was located and where they hoped were the best chances for work. They got there late on Saturday.

Early Monday morning, Uncle Abdon, Eugène and Maurice joined a long lineup under an increasingly hot sun. At nine o'clock, someone came out of the Personnel Office to tell them that the Manager would not be back before one o'clock. The men decided to stay in the lineup, anyway.

Around four o'clock, Maurice got in George McNaughton's office. He could tell the Personnel Manager wanted him out of the office as soon as possible. Maurice was dehydrated, a bit stressed out but determined to have his say – but what can you say when you have a grade six education and no special skills to offer?

"Can you read and write?" McNaughton asked.

"Yes," he answered. "I only went to our village school but two years ago I took some courses at St. Francis Xavier University, in Nova Scotia", he added proudly.

"You did! Well, I may have something for you here," he said as he reached into a box and pulled out a small card that he held up in front of Maurice's face.

"This is the National Registration Card for war service. It'll be used for everything from now on: coupons for sugar, butter and so on; and for information on everyone's whereabouts. Do you think you could fill these out in legible handwriting?"

"I am sure I can do that work to your satisfaction, sir."

"Tomorrow morning, at eight o'clock, report to the office next door. You'll join up with a group of university and college students about to canvas every part of town and register everyone in sight."

Maurice mumbled words of thanks and sort of floated out of the office, the happiest man in the whole Province of Quebec.

For the next thee weeks he worked as part of a 16-member crew to fill out the registration cards. He took it upon himself to follow very strict standards of clear legible writing and good spelling. He made special efforts to communicate with those who spoke neither English nor French (many recent immigrants had chosen the Saguenay region and hadn't had time to adapt).

This special care towards the newcomers helped to confirm his job, he believes, as, after a few days, he was assigned to deal mostly with them. Needless to say, he met a lot of people, quickly learned his way around town and got to explore the paper mill thoroughly – he even climbed the woodpiles (about 300 feet) using the pulp trolley, to register everyone and not cause lost work time.

Once the registration drive was completed, Mr. McNaughton decided to assign Maurice to the paper inspection team. He told the young man to report to Mr. Wishart.

"Pay careful attention to everything he says because he's not easy. And speak loudly, he's hard of hearing."

The noise inside the mill was deafening. Everything seemed to vibrate and communications closely resembled a lip-reading exercise. After a brief exchange, Mr. Wishart tapped him on the shoulder.

"Be here at eight tomorrow morning, we'll start your training."

Shift work was hard. Night shifts were a major challenge. Moreover, there was a policy that, if your replacement didn't show up for work, you had to stay on the job an extra four hours to give Personnel time to re-adjust the schedule; a 12-hour shift was supreme misery.

One of these 12-hour shifts was particularly difficult. Maurice could hardly keep his eyes open when he realized a set of paper rolls was missing. The full rolls were cut in smaller sizes according to the customer's order. For example, one full roll could be cut into two 36-inch, one 18-inch, and one 22-inch roll. To him it looked as if they were missing one complete set.

He was worried. Mr. Lepage, the foreman, was a tall muscular individual who knew his job and valued his good standing with the company. He was proud of his crew. A newcomer could not walk up to him and say flatly someone had made a mistake, few could be that daring. If he were wrong, at best he would get a blast; at worst, they would stop the machine and cause the company to lose money over such a mistake.

But he had to act, and act fast. So, shaking in his boots, Maurice went to Lepage and told him that it was possible that production was short one set of rolls on an order. Lepage ran to the shipping area to count the rolls. He was back in a minute and came directly to Maurice.

"You were right," he said. "Luckily for us, we only have to re-adjust the cutters; we don't have to stop the machine. Good work, Maurice."

That's how he qualified as a member of the paper inspection team.

After about six months, Maurice was called for military service. This first experience with the army was everything you don't care to write home about: basic training without uniform or gear; and tests for intelligence, personality and aptitudes. After 30 days, the men were put on a waiting list and sent home.

Maurice's old job wasn't waiting for him and money was dwindling fast. Regularly, he would drop in at the Personnel Office at Price Brothers. He knew several employees in that office but, more importantly, he knew Mr. McNaughton, the manager.

After a few weeks, Mr. McNaughton called Maurice to his office.

"There's a job available right now," he said. "But I don't think you'll want it."

"It would have to be a pretty bad job, for me to turn it down."

"It's a cleaning and maintenance job at the company staff house."

"I'll take it. When do I start?"

"I must warn you. You'll be working for Mrs. Baxter, the most disagreeable person I've ever met. She usually screams and swears at everyone. Check it out and, if you turn the job down, I certainly won't hold that against you."

Mrs. Baxter's reputation was well deserved; nevertheless, he stayed there for three months.

On August 6, 1941, our brother Roméo married a girl from Les Iles-de-la-Madeleine. For the occasion, my parents made the trip to their birthplace which they had left in 1913. They were all expected to return to Baie-Ste-Anne for the following week; so, with Louis and Adéodat, Dad's two half-brothers, Maurice left the Saguenay to join the family in New Brunswick.

Soon after his arrival home, Maurice told my father he was determined to join the army as soon as he got back to the Saguenay.

"Sign up here, in Newcastle," Dad suggested. "Don't bother to go back to Quebec."

"I discovered that speaking both French and English gave me some advantages in Quebec," Maurice said.

The following Monday morning, he reported to the army recruitment office. He was the first one there, so the clerk, thinking he'd been up all night, suggested he might have had quite a drunken weekend.

"I'm here to enlist. If you don't want me, I'll leave and won't bother you anymore," the tee-totalling Maurice replied.

The paperwork was quickly over with and his medical was a mere formality. Then, he had to pass an eye examination. He was worried that he would be turned down as his eyesight was rather poor. Just as he entered Dr. George William Tremblay's office, the doctor was called out in the hall. Maurice spotted the eye test chart, walked over and, as he has an excellent memory, he took time to study the chart. When the doctor returned, Maurice read line after line perfectly, with both eyes. For the first and only time in his entire life, he had 20/20 vision!

In those days when you worked for a company, they owned you, especially a big outfit like Price. The Quebec Royal Rifles was the preferred unit for company employees but Maurice figured that, though he worked for Price, he wouldn't join The Quebec Royal Rifles. A wise decision since that regiment was sent to Hong Kong and the men endured years of misery and starvation as prisoners of war.

On Labor Day weekend, Maurice left his job once more and travelled to Quebec City. The military was waiting for him. True to their motto "Hurry up and wait", the men were paraded for uniforms, bedding, mess kits, etc. On the next parade, his name was called out and he was told to report to the Pay Office.

The Paymaster, Company Sergeant Major LeHoullier, looked him over.

"I guess you'll be working here from now on."

"There must be some mistake."

"No mistake. Your test results indicate that you have a place here."

There were several fresh recruits starting out on the job and CSM LeHoullier put them through an intensive training schedule over and above their regular workload. Maurice didn't feel he could fit very well with the group as he had no training on the typewriter. He was told to go down town and buy a typewriting method book. For the next several weeks, he worked as a file clerk and learned typing in his spare time. A month later, he was able to replace a full time typist.

At first they had to study an army manual called Financial Regulations and Instructions. CSM LeHoullier gave them lectures on the subject and they were given an exam.

The group was made up of bank clerks and accountants. Maurice didn't feel that he could compete with such a group of well-educated men but, when the results were announced, he was at the top! Some of them were humiliated but they got used to it as he came first in all subsequent tests. No doubt the fact that he was more familiar with the English language accounted for much, as legal jargon in any language tends to carry its own heavy dose of confusion.

The Pay Office was his workplace for three years.

He eventually developed extreme back pain. The doctor diagnosed tuberculosis of the spine. In August 1944, he was sent to the Lancaster Hospital in Saint John to be closer to home. He was there for one month. At that time the first casualties of the Normandy Invasion were coming home for treatment.

One day my brother Cyrille came to visit him. They discussed his options as the army would discharge him as soon as he left the hospital.

"I may be overly ambitious," he said. "Do you think I could take a Cost Accounting course?"

"How do you plan to carry that out?"

"I'd like to register at the Success Business College in Moncton and follow a program especially designed to meet my needs. I don't want to join up with the rest, some of whom are not motivated and just make things drag on."

"I'll see what I can do," said Cyrille.

My brother, Fr. Cyrille D'Amour, could sometimes do some amazing things to help us along the way. In this case, he contacted Mr. England who was a Career Counselor for the military. Mr. England had been one of Cyrille's teachers at the Newcastle elementary school.

"My brother wants to take a Cost Accounting course but he lacks the basic academic certification. How complicated is that?" inquired Cyrille.

Shortly after, Maurice met with Mr. England. He had drawn up a special 30-day agreement that would see him expelled from the school if he failed the tests. Moreover, because of the failure, he would be excluded from any support from the military should he later decide to further his education.

Courses began immediately and, throughout, he suffered debilitating back pains. However, 30 days later, Mr. Mac D. Cooke, Principal of the college, congratulated him on having successfully covered a 45-day course equivalent. He was then duly registered with the veterans' program and, 10 months later, he graduated proudly from the Success Business College having completed the 18-month training program. And so began his financial career.

With the Air Force
Antonio D'Amour

My brother Ludger became a monk in 1937. I
suspect that in 1940 my mother wrote to him begging
him to find something for François because his twin
careers as lumberjack and fisherman were on the
rocks. He wasn't aware of these transactions, however,
when he received a letter from Ludger advising him
that there was possible employment where he was
posted at *Collège Saint-Laurent* in Montreal.

There, François was initiated to carpentry and
he worked hard for his $25 per month. He enjoyed
his time with Ludger. And, since the older brother
was now a master carpenter and was involved in
various interesting construction and repair projects,
François took advantage of the situation to pick up
the tricks of the trade and to develop into a competent carpenter helper.

Canada was at war. Victory Bond drives became
important social gathering events that in turn helped
enlistment in the military. He attended one of these
rallies in late November, 1941, in Montreal where he

met with recruiting officers for the Royal Canadian Air Force and decided to enlist.

"Freezing weather is here and I can't afford winter clothes, so I signed up with the Air Force." he told Ludger.

A few days later, he got a call to report to the Manning Depot in Quebec City. That same morning he was at the Bonaventure Station waiting for the train. It was a busy scene with hundreds of young men in uniform heading off in all directions. The public address system crackled, sputtered and barked:

"Attention everybody. We have just been told that the Japanese have attacked Pearl Harbor."

That got everyone's attention. Everywhere in the station complete strangers were talking to each other in very animated conversations. What an ice-breaker that was! Most of them had no idea where Pearl Harbor was located but in a few short days the whole North American population was deeply immersed in the geography of the Pacific and the treachery of the Japanese government. And, to the obvious relief of the allied forces, the United States was now fighting mad.

At the Manning Depot in Quebec City, they went through medical, shots, IQ tests, uniform and kit issues, basic training, and job assignment. Everything was quick, short, confusing, and inadequate for practical military service

They ended up in Mont-Joli. The base was a work in progress. Since it was January, the drafty barracks were heated with coal-burning pot-bellied stoves with a long pipe going out the window. In the morning all the men were black

Although François was assigned to temporary duty in various locations, Mont-Joli was to be his home base for the duration of the war.

In 1942, German U-boats made incursions up the St. Lawrence River. Rumours placed them everywhere and villagers along the coast claimed to have had German-speaking visitors mingle with them at the local weekend dances. The new recruits were assigned to security patrols. The basic training provided at the Manning Depot had not qualified any of them for that job. François had no idea what to do with his rifle, having never fired a shot. Nevertheless, they did sentinel duty with no further training and fortunately the Germans never found out our state of non-readiness.

After a few weeks, they were provided with a sort of script for the rules of engagement, in case anyone with hostile intentions came within range.

"Who goes there?"
"Advance and be recognized."
If the individual is recognized, okay; if not bark "Halt!"
Re-enforce the command with a shot in the air.
Should the individual refuse to stop.
Shoot to kill.

The best plans of the top brass had overlooked the fact that many of the men could not speak the King's English; so, ludicrous dialogues took place where the sentinel would confuse "Who goes there?" with "Who am I" and so on. By staying in their humid U-boats, I believe many a German sailor missed out on a very good Keystone Cops comedy.

François decided to buy a radio. So, he started saving small amounts of money and, deposits of one or two dollars were beginning to add up. Then a letter came from my mother saying my little sister Maria needed glasses; really, he didn't want the radio that much, anyway.

After a while he was assigned to manage the Snack Bar. Corporal Gustave Faniel the Phys-Ed instructor was a good friend and he was known for his successes with the girls. One day, he told François there was a newcomer at the Records Office.

"Check her out, Frank," he suggested. "As a matter of fact, she was here at the Snack Bar last night. You must've noticed her, she was wearing a red coat."

That evening, there she was. François was introduced to Denise Chénier and they became very good friends. It was early spring 1944.

A few weeks later, he started having pains in his right side and the doctor decided to remove his appendix. The operation took place on June 6, 1944 (D-Day). When he woke up after surgery, Denise was there to check on him with a friend of hers, Grace Dubé. Little did he know at the time that Denise and he would marry on June 20, 1945.

L'Évangéline

Roméo D'Amour

Cyrille again came to my rescue in mid-August, 1942. "Archbishop Robichaud is looking for someone to take over the position of Manager at L'Évangéline. Go to Moncton and try your luck." L'Évangéline was the Acadian newspaper. I rushed to Moncton and met with the Archbishop. We had an excellent meeting and I landed the job. He tried to prepare me for the board, office and staff politics of particular concern and I felt confident that, with his support, I could handle the work involved.

We moved to Moncton and found a small apartment where we settled for a possible short stay considering the war and the precarious financial situation of the newspaper.

Alfred Roy was the editor. I believe we hit it off quite well and he proceeded to provide me with the essential information for my new start in a completely foreign milieu. I met with the staff and noted that this condition of living on the edge of financial disaster had seriously dampened their spirit. To them every tomorrow was a threatening Doomsday.

I immersed myself in the newspaper publishing and commercial printing business. I wanted a good basic knowledge of the industry before everyone realized that I knew nothing about it. I met several times with the Board of Directors; I had frequent discussions with the editor and with the plant superintendent.

I studied the past history of L'Évangéline. I attempted to analyze the cycles of ups and downs to get a better grasp of the route we were following; I drew up lists of past, recent and present problems in view of planning for the future. I was in deep water and forced, for a while, to sort of dogpaddle.

There were seven people on the editorial and office staff: the editor, the assistant-editor-translator, the secretary, the bookkeeper, two journalists and the receptionist. In the plant: a superintendent, a press foreman, a bindery foreman and the plant personnel – in total, 29 employees.

For the next three months, I planned to get fully acquainted with the mechanics of the newspaper business, more particularly the ways things were done at L'Évangéline. When they realized that I wasn't about to disrupt the routine, the employees became relaxed, confident and cooperative. They willingly provided me with inside knowledge of their activities.

I traveled to The Telegraph-Journal in Saint John and to The Halifax Chronicle-Herald in Halifax to study how other plants operated and to see, with envy, their much more advanced equipment. With the help of management, in both cities, I made up lists of essential books and manuals on composition, printing presses, bindery operations and job estimates. My evenings and weekends became on-going study sessions.

By the end of July, I was confident that I could begin my move to streamline operations. I purchased a re-conditioned paper folder to replace our antique hand-fed machine. I got two dummy linotype keyboards to train our operators. Then came time for a Multilith offset press to begin the gradual conversion from letterpress to offset printing. When I revised the estimating procedures with the unwilling participation of the plant superintendent, it was felt I was rocking the boat. And, sometimes, I was met with passive and occasionally active resistance.

Whether by design or accident, I was put to the test.

One Monday morning, Bud, our best and most competent compositor, failed to report for work. As I was going home for lunch, I met him on Main Street, drunk as the proverbial skunk. I asked him when I could expect him back to work. He took the opportunity to provide me with a more or less coherent list of his problems and, for supplement, he offered a rather dull review of the past 50 years of his life. I hadn't asked for so much.

"Bud, come in tomorrow morning and I'll forget this. Now, go home and sleep it off."

"Mr. D'Amour, I couldn't sleep if off if I tried. See... I'm shaking like a leaf. I need two dollars for a good drink to steady my nerves and then I might be able to sleep it off."

"Here's two dollars, Bud. I'll see you at eight tomorrow."

Bud didn't show up the next morning. There were 15 ads to be set up for the next day and it seemed to me that the plant superintendent acted as though it was my problem and not his.

"The paper will be out Wednesday morning. We have the rest of the morning, this afternoon and tonight to get most of the work done. Tuesday, we'll tie up loose ends. In short, tonight, neither I, nor you, nor your composition staff is leaving the place until 90 per cent of the ads are set. Hedging and pussy-footing time is over. Let's get to work."

Five minutes after I had left for lunch, Bud walked in and asked the bookkeeper for a $10 advance on his pay.

"Sorry, the manager isn't here at the moment."

"I know, I just saw him and he told me to get the money from you."

"Sorry again, Bud, but Mr. D'Amour has to tell me that personally."

"Are you calling me a liar? Get that petty cash box here, right now, or I'll get it myself."

When he heard the commotion, Alfred Roy, the editor, came out of his office to investigate. When Alfred showed up, Bud walked out.

We finished the ads at 2:30 p.m. but I still had a long day ahead of me. At seven o'clock, I was at my desk when Bud entered the building. The receptionist intercepted him and, as instructed, directed him to my office.

"Sit down, Bud."

"I prefer to stand up."

"Bud, you've caused quite a few problems lately. Monday morning, you didn't show up for work so everyone else had to pick up the slack. Today, you sneaked in after I left with a made-up story and you tried to scare the secretary into giving you ten dollars. Then you ran off when Alfred showed up. We've learned a few things in your last visits, Bud: you're a liar, a thief and a coward. What are we going to learn this time?"

"The last guy who spoke to me like that got my hand across the mouth."

I rounded my desk and walked up to him in defiance. He raised his fist. I grabbed him by the shoulders and pitched him out of my office and against the counter, where he collapsed.

"Oh, my God, he killed Bud," the receptionist cried. For the past 17 years Bud had been the top compositor at L'Évangéline. He was a wizard in a very specialized field. He had gradually been given the impression that he could get away with anything. He was led to believe that his periodic drinking bouts with ensuing absenteeism would be tolerated no matter what.

"I knew that sooner or later something like this would happen," said the Archbishop. "I must call a meeting of the Board to discuss this matter immediately. Meanwhile, try to relax."

Bud's firing was approved at the meeting.

I called a general meeting of the personnel to explain the situation and to ask for their cooperation in trying to adjust to working without Bud. I told them that if they had suggestions, comments or grievances "my door is always open".

The following week, Moncton was hit with an incredible heat wave. Everyone was miserable. We had no air-conditioning. We slowed the pace.

At noon on Wednesday, Alfred invited me to his office. Our weekly paper had just been printed and everyone was in a happy mood. Thomas, his assistant, came in for a chat. Alfred offered me a drink "to cool me off". I politely refused pointing out that "I don't touch liquor during office hours". We talked for a few more minutes and I left for home.

The following morning, Thomas did not show up for work. Alfred came in, visibly very sick. In the afternoon we were informed that Thomas had been taken to hospital – he was blind! He died at 7 p.m.

At 8:30, I tried to locate Alfred. Finally I found out he had been taken from his office to the hospital. I rushed over. At 10 o'clock he was blind and he died during the night.

In the morning, two police officers were with me when I opened the door at the newspaper. I escorted them directly to Alfred's office. On his typewriter was a white sheet of paper on which was written:

"We are sorry to announce the death of a dear friend and co-worker, J. Thomas..."

Alfred had been unable to complete the text.

Tchaikovsky's Fifth

Antonio D'Amour

I realized I had been tricked. It was obvious to me now. He had set the scene, moved in the shadows to wait patiently and I had walked unaware into his trap. I stopped my bike on the side of the road, on Arran Street hill, and leaned forward on the handlebars. I had to think this through.

It was November, 1946, and I was 13 years old. My parents had moved to Campbellton just in time for the school year. That's when I got to know my older brother Cyrille. When I was born, he was in college, as I grew up he was in Seminary. He suffered from bleeding stomach ulcers. He seldom dared come home to Baie-Ste-Anne because it was far from hospitals and doctors. I knew Cyrille was the eldest of the family, 20 years my senior. I knew he was a priest... and not much else.

Cyrille measured about 5 ft. 10 in. He was a bit thin at the time because he was recuperating from a stomach operation. He had a generous smile that came easily as he enjoyed meeting people. He loved to play the flute and the oboe. I can still picture him standing in front of his little music stand playing his beautiful silver flute, his black robe swaying to the rhythm of Schubert's *Serenade* or the *Chinese Dance* from the Nutcracker Suite.

At that time, he lived in a small lovely apartment at the Hotel-Dieu Hospital where he was Chaplain. His friends were all those sick people and their families who felt they needed him and the inner peace his ministry represented. His other friends were doctors, lawyers, musicians, artists and authors and they often came to visit him.

Cyrille must have been intrigued when he met me. I was developing into a strong healthy boy who had excellent marks in school and, like all the boys my age, I had no inkling of what the future had to offer. I loved going to his place because he was interesting and so were his many friends but I particularly enjoyed the fact that he encouraged me whenever I expressed an interest in something.

Since Europe was in reconstruction because of the devastation caused by World War Two, a lot of interesting news reports put a positive spin on mankind's creativity. It was a new vocation for reporters who had glorified and promoted savagery and senseless destruction.

At this time, the Berlin Library had suffered greatly from Allied bombings and there was a feature in one of the newspapers on what was being done to preserve and restore the documents. I thought that weekly column was very interesting and, one day, I asked Cyrille to tell me about bookbinding.

His eyes lit up. Immediately he gave me an impromptu lecture on the subject. Then he promised me a lot more information in the near future. I don't think I had asked quite as much, but anyway...

The following week, while I was in school he learned from a monk at the Restigouche Monastery how to take apart old books and sew them back together. He had one of my brothers build two small stands for sewing and he designed a complex vise to hold books of any size for the application of glue, cotton backing and other processes. He was ready for the weekend.

We took several old damaged books from the hospital library and went to work. Soon, they were all taken apart in small booklets, the old thread and cracked glue were carefully removed and each damaged page was repaired as best we could. Almost 60 years later, I can still enjoy the neat and classy appearance of some of our work on precious books.

Because I loved drawing and sketching, he enrolled me in a well-designed correspondence course with The Washington School of Art and this initial training has provided me with thousands of enjoyable hours over decades with a sketch book or in front of an easel.

From his good friend, Dr. Ernest Dumont, he borrowed a cello and just left it there next to the little sofa. I knew he wanted me to ask questions but I was afraid I'd have to learn to play that strange looking instrument, so I kept quiet, for a while. But whenever he would leave me alone in his apartment, I'd experiment with it. One day, Cyrille caught me and, for the next couple of years, I took lessons from Mrs. Sharp, a kind and gifted musician who was condemned to teaching children with little talent for 50 cents an hour.

I liked Cyrille. He was fun to be with. He was a walking encyclopedia on everything. Meals with him were tasty and generous but it was the conversation that charmed me. Without effort he would dazzle me with three-minute lectures on anything and everything: philosophy, astronomy, music, art, horseracing, navigation, history, psychology and photography. With him I met bald-headed Greek philosophers, hairy musicians of the 18th and 19th centuries, flashy orchestra conductors of our times, mule-headed architects and engineers, and the wonderful writers that chronicled mankind's evolution.

We got along fine on most things but I deplored his taste in music. For many weeks, his record player growled the same monotonous music that he proudly identified as Tchaikovsky's Symphony No. 5 in E minor. My choices were more in keeping with the times: *Third Man Theme* with Guy Lombardo or *Tonight We Love* with Freddy Martin, good stuff with an air and a beat. I felt secure that, with his draggy tunes, especially the first two records, he could never find any arguments to get me to listen to classical music – after all a young man has the right to listen to what he likes.

But I never got to argue the point with him and he never mentioned why he felt the need to play that weird music. That was the shock. I had surprised myself humming those damn Tchaikovsky tunes and unconsciously enjoying them!

I jumped on the pedals and headed downhill at top speed trying to shake that music out of my head, hoping to generate a wind tunnel effect that would forever erase those tunes from my repertoire. It didn't work. I guess you don't expel Tchaikovsky from your head with a breeze, even if you can pedal as fast as a 13-year-old.

Sometimes I wonder why he didn't try to trap me with Schubert's *The Trout*, Rimsky-Korsakov's *Flight of the Bumblebee* or Beethoven's *Fur Elise*. He must have known I could discover these desserts on my own.

First, he wanted me to acquire a taste for Tchaikovsky's veggies. And it had worked quite well.

L'Île D'Amour
Antonio D'Amour

François owns a small island in the Baie-des-Chaleurs. It's been his now for more than four decades. Every year he spends about six months in his humble chalet where family and old friends come on annual visits, where new and lasting friendships are formed. It's something of a magic place; here quiet dreams float by carried on the mists of the bay and, at times in the distance, a centuries-old phantom ship burns brightly, bemoaning a pirate's deed.

Twenty years ago the government took over a small segment of his paradise to build a new wharf for the local fishermen. Then they built a causeway making *l'île D'Amour* a peninsula – some bureaucrats are like Atilla's horse, nothing must take root in their hoofprints.

But he discovered long ago that, causeway be damned, his island still holds the heady scents of romance and the greenish hues of mystery; so, *l'île D'Amour* lives on.

He never planned to own an island. Circumstances gave it to him and it's been a perfect refuge from the madding crowd.

In 1960, François took over the job of Sheriff of Restigouche County, New Brunswick. Among his responsibilities, he had to deal with arrears in school and property taxes. It was a job that he carried out as humanely as possible.

One winter day in 1961, he was asked to tack a "For Sale" sign on an old shack located on a small island. He crossed over at low tide. The shack was in bad shape. The owner had died leaving behind a decade of unpaid taxes. On impulse he checked the total tax bill: $11.

The shack was scheduled to be auctioned off a week later. On that day, Dalhousie experienced a major snowstorm. At the appointed time, no one showed up for the auction.

"I'll buy it." he told the county clerk and quickly paid the eleven dollars.

He was also required to pay ten dollars for arrears on the lease of the island and then he was informed that the annual school tax amounted to eleven cents.

Every year, he promptly settled his 11-cent tax bill. One day he noticed a small footnote that informed taxpayers of a 10% deduction that would be made on any bill paid in full within 30 days. For some reason the Secretary to the School Board, Atherton Taylor, categorically refused to honour that rule for François..

Leasing was fine but now he wanted to buy "his island". He found out that in order for his request to be considered, he would have to make an offer to the Department of Natural Resources for them to exchange the island for property adjacent to Crown Lands. My brother Cyrille owned such a property in the village of Beaver Brook. The deal was soon made and the island was granted to François D'Amour, thus *L'Île D'Amour*. His children and grandchildren all have special personal reasons to visit the island every summer. Some come for a few hours, many for an overnight visit and several for longer stays either with François and Denise in the cottage or in tents on the east point. Cyrille enjoyed a few short years of retirement in a mobile home that he had installed near them. He spent many happy hours in his small sailboat, travelling with the winds and tides from l'Île D'Amour to Heron Island about half a mile out in the Baie-des-Chaleurs.

Edith Butler, the famous Acadian folksinger spent many a carefree hour there, sometimes looking for agates, sometimes just sitting on a rocky promontory and staring out to sea. I like to believe that the Muses were present to inspire some of her beautiful songs.

Our brother Julien and his wife Denise often came with their children to the island for their summer vacation. It was there that Mike, about ten years old at the time, learned to row a boat and test his sailing skills. Lynne, Christine and Charlene learned a lot about feeding ever-hungry gulls and they enjoyed endless hours at their favorite playground sport of scaling the five-foot geodesic dome assembled with one-inch aluminum pipes by their uncle Cyrille. Three-year-old Daniel, now an RCMP officer, carried out his first investigations on that rocky terrain

Throughout the years, visitors to the island carried away many wonderful memories. One example comes to mind.

There was this American friend, Richard Maddox, who for some years was with the US Air Force at Loring Air Base, ME. He later moved to Florida. Richard loved to come for a few days every year and have the island for himself, his wife and some friends. On the shoreline he would replenish his supply of agates as his hobby was making jewelry.

One year he arrived earlier than usual. It was a cold and rainy day when they stopped at François' to pick up the key. They were two couples. François was a bit concerned for their comfort.

"You'll have to wait a few hours for the tide to come down; so, you may as well have supper with us and I'll go with you to make sure everything is alright." he said.

It was dark when they drove over the sand bar and got on the island.

The chalet hadn't been used for months. A lively fire was lit in the old Star kitchen stove. A few oil lamps pushed back the shadows. Then the women discovered the old Victrola gramophone.

Radios or other noise boxes were not allowed on the island. Old books of Conan Doyle stories, Treasure Island, well-worn copies of Reader's Digest Condensed Books along with a few very old National Geographic magazines provided entertainment on rainy days.

As the men sat in front of the fire, the two women went through the limited collection of old 78-rpm records. They cranked up the mechanism and the happy scratchy tune of "I Have a Gal in Galveston" played. Richard and his wife got up to dance as the other lady came over to her husband crying like a baby.

"What's the problem?" François asked.

"Oh. Nothing... But, believe it or not, she's really a gal from Galveston." he said as he held her in his arms.

Once again the magic of *L'Île D'Amour* had taken effect.

Safety in the Workplace

Antonio D'Amour

When François got off the plane in Oran, Algeria, it was late afternoon. Parsons-Whitmore from New York had hired him to give safety training to the employees of a new papermill that they had built a short distance from the port city. Midland-Ross had sent an engineer, a paper dryer specialist by the name of Don MacAnesty from Montreal, to train maintenance personnel for their equipment. A man from the local mill was to meet them and help them get set up for a fairly long stay.

Algeria is a francophone country; so, when François' name was called over the PA system, he recognized it immediately. He reported to the reception desk and there he was greeted by a tall and slim Algerian who asked him where the other Canadian was. François didn't know. The Algerian took the microphone and called out a very unlikely series of sounds that had no resemblance with any name

François had ever heard in Canada. He looked over his host's shoulder; the name was Don MacAnesty, a rather difficult moniker for a North African, no doubt.

He picked up the microphone and called out Don's name and they looked around trying to spot him in the crowd. There was a commotion to the right towards the back. They looked and spotted a man in a sort of cage, a holding cell. He was gesticulating, jumping up and down as if determined to attract attention. They went to him. He hadn't thought of getting a visa and, in those paranoid countries, you'd better have all your papers on you all the time.

After a bit of palaver and officious bureaucratic verbal exchanges, he was finally released under François' direct responsibility. Don was very grateful as he had feared for his life having been treated like a criminal by so many armed security guards.

Their guide took them to their apartment. It was a new development, a showcase section of town where the government of the day would demonstrate how much they cared for their average countrymen. They were definitely true to their word; it was an unequivocal statement on the relationship between the government and the average citizen.

The place was on the second floor. Their Algerian guide opened the door and they walked in. There were crunching noises as if they were walking on corn flakes; they looked down and the place was crawling with cockroaches, a true moving carpet. His mission accomplished, the guide left

The two Canadians looked around and burst out laughing. Cautiously they draped their coats on top of the doors, placed the suitcases on chairs and walked about murdering without mercy hundreds of cockroaches as they inspected the place. It was late afternoon and, after this introduction to Algerian hospitality, they decided to explore for food – very cautiously. There wasn't a bite to eat in the place.

"I have a bottle of gin," François said.

"I'll get the glasses."

There were no glasses, so they settled for the cover of an underarm deodorant container. To the castanet sounds of crushing cockroaches underfoot, the men returned to the kitchen for water only to discover that the tap was dry. They didn't sleep that first night and the bottle of gin proved a worthy travel companion.

The papermill was new. Everything looked fine. François wondered why, with only one papermaking machine, they felt they needed 800 employees but this was a different world. In Canada, four-machine mills employed fewer than 400 men and produced 1000 tons of paper per day. Here, seven tons.

He began his safety training seminars and workshops and enjoyed the experience very much. The men were interested, asked questions and willingly took part in the demonstrations. He felt they were making some progress and, after a few days, he began to come to work feeling somewhat upbeat.

"We've lost a man," the foreman reported one morning.

"What happened?"

"He fell off the roof and died instantly."

"How can that be? Everyone sent to work in high places is required to use a safety rope."

"He had a rope."

François went to the scene of the accident. True, the man was dead. He had fallen about 50 feet. He checked and the poor fellow did have a rope around his waist. He went up and, sure enough, the other end was firmly anchored to a steel bracket near the edge of the roof – the fatal error – the rope measured 60 feet!

There were other hazards. The plants used in the paper-making process were harvested off the mountain sides. The work was done by state convicts who were paid a stipend per ton. They generously contributed rocks and other extra weighty materials but their most dangerous items with the truckloads were venomous snakes. A team of snake exterminators was on duty every day.

It was difficult to preach the use of steel-toed boots as every one who bothered with footwear preferred the classic rubber boot. Many went barefoot and he once observed a worker in rubber boots busy cutting a section off a large steel beam. Sparks of molten steel flew everywhere and his barefoot helper was kept hopping.

Some of the more prosperous workers traveled to work by scooter. It soon became apparent that these vehicles were an added hazard as the men didn't trust their co-workers and carried the scooters on their backs wherever they had to work, sometimes up three stories.

While François was in Algeria, Canada was hosting the '67 Olympics. Every evening, many of the men would travel to nearby Oran to watch the events on TV. The next day they would tell him about the rich and colourful Canadian scenery; they would marvel at the greenery, the water and the wonderful city of Montreal.

Three weeks after his arrival, Ramadan, the ninth month of the Muslim year, began and that put an end to his work in Algeria. He took the plane to Paris where, because of the heavy traffic between France and Canada due to the Olympics, he had to wait four days before he could get a seat on Air Canada. Having to spend four days in that great city without an assigned program and with all expenses paid did not cause him any undue stress.

That first night, he unpacked his suitcase, hung his clothes in the closet, walked across a quiet floor, had a relaxing shower and slept. His Paris hotel room was all the more appealing after his Algerian experience.

Blessings of the Poor
Ludger D'Amour

On Christmas Eve 1956, we were living in St. Bonaventure parish in Ottawa. We had four children. There were two Christmas masses, one at midnight and another in the morning, at 10 o'clock.

My wife Gertrude would stay at home with the children in the evening so that I could attend midnight mass. In the morning, with the two older girls, Hélène six and Cécile four, she would go to church while I stayed at home with the younger ones, Jean-Marie who was three and Martine only fifteen months.

Our Christmas celebration, at 1400 Raven Street, included a Christmas story in front of the fireplace, a few forty-five rpm records of Christmas music and a polka. The entertainment and music were my share of the parental education.

I had set up the Christmas tree with a few decorations from past years and a few splats of plaster of Paris to imitate snow. We had placed a gift for each one under the tree as well as individual Christmas cards with a personal love message.

As we lived a short distance from the church, I set out on foot to go to Midnight Mass. I enjoyed the weather and marvelled at the beautiful decorations of the richer homes along the way. When I got close to the church, I was approached by a young man with a beard who asked me to help him and his family have a decent Christmas. I had a five dollar bill in my pocket, my Christmas collection money. On the spur of the moment, without questioning or judging the gentleman beggar, I handed him the five dollars.

He was very polite with me wishing me a Merry Christmas and added so sincerely, "God will bless you."

I had one dollar left for the church collection and we had all we needed at the house to celebrate.

Next morning, the early to bed were the early to rise and, even before breakfast, the wrappings were stripped off and everyone enjoyed their gifts and their messages of love. I thought of the simple tranquillity of my young family, enjoying the warm atmosphere of a home where love was shared by everyone and no one had a worry in the world. Was this the blessing offered by the gentleman beggar the night before? I assumed it was.

Life continued with the occasional worry about health and periods of financial insecurity, but we managed to survive and we moved to Montreal two years later. Ten years later, the children were all in school and the company I worked for closed down its construction department, so I was out of work. I tried selling equipment but it didn't pay enough to support my growing family.

I longed to start a business of my own. I had an idea I could make money manufacturing steel shelving for grocery stores. I had no experience in sheet metal work and the equipment to do the job was much more than I could afford. I tried to borrow money from two banks but was turned down. With no where to turn, I went to a high interest finance company to borrow the required capital. With my balance sheet and my lack of experience, I knew that, even there, my chances of getting a loan were slim. I wanted seven thousand dollars to be repaid over three years.

Next day, I got the answer by phone; my loan was granted. The first three years were not easy but my business survived. When I went to make my last loan payment, I asked the manager what made him decide to loan me the money in the first place, since I had so little collateral. He would not tell me; he just smiled and said, "Sometimes small things can make a big difference."

My business developed into a successful venture and supported my family very well. For many years, I forgot about that Christmas Eve in Ottawa, the blessing of the gentleman beggar and my unexpected loan.

Last week, more than 45 years after the fact, I had a dream of those years of struggle and hardship. In my dream, I met two men, neither one had a beard. They came smiling to me and one told me his friend knew me from a long time ago when he was a beggar on a certain Christmas Eve in Ottawa. He said that his friend had gotten the job of manager in a finance company and he had recognized me when I had applied for a loan.

Now I wonder: was this a dream or was it my subconscious working out a mystery that had stayed with me for so many years?

It would explain why I was granted that loan and it would explain the manager's comment, "Sometimes small things can make a big difference."

It would also explain the blessings of the poor... but, maybe, blessings need no explanation.

The Lure of the Maggies

Donna D'Amour

Ever since I met Tony, he's talked about visiting the Magdalen Islands in the Gulf of St.Lawrence, not only because of their natural beauty but also because of his personal connection to the island archipelago. Tony's grandfather, Louis D'Amour, left his home in France at age 14 and joined the French navy. Two years later, his ship Le Zenobi arrived at the Islands. When she returned to France, Louis stayed behind. A deserter in the eyes of France, he never dared to return – not even for a visit – and he never saw his home again.

Louis eventually became captain of a trading schooner called the Alice Mae. In 1887, he was shipwrecked by a fierce winter gale on Sandy Hook, a sandbar off the Magdalen Islands. He and his crew lashed themselves to the masts while the islanders tried in vain to reach them. After two days, the storm died down and the islanders were able to cut them free. The men were frozen in blocks of ice and were taken to thaw out by kitchen stoves. Amazingly, every man survived.

In June 2000, my husband Tony and I finally got the chance to take what would be a sentimental journey to the islands. We went with Tony's brother Ludger and his wife Henriette to see for ourselves what had captivated grandfather Louis and countless other visitors over time.

Les Îles-de-la-Madeleine, or Magdalen Islands, are located in the Gulf of St.Lawrence and are part of Quebec, although they are part of the Atlantic time zone, one hour ahead of the rest of the province. There are twelve islands in all; seven are connected by long, thin sand dunes. The main highway is bordered by dunes that make for continuous photo opportunities.

As our ferry neared l'Île d'Entrée at the southern entrance of the archipelago, the wind was cold but the sun shone brightly. The terrain of this small island rises and falls so dramatically it looks as if its hills have been sculpted by hand. Only 178 people live there and, because it isn't linked to the other islands, residents must travel by boat or plane.

We got off the ferry at Cap-aux-Meules. It's almost sunset as we climb the many steps to the lookout. It's the golden hour and a warm light covers the harbour and the houses dotting the coast. From here we drive north to Havre-aux-Maisons, about midpoint in the chain of islands.

It takes less than an hour to drive from Havre-Aubert to the southern tip of Grosse-Île and Grande-Entrée in the north – only if you don't stop to admire the view.

Our rented house in Cap-Rouge, on the north shore of Havre-aux-Maisons, sits atop red cliffs sheltering nesting swallows. The next morning we set out to explore. The colors are breath-taking: red cliffs carved by wind and waves, tall pillars of red sandstone on white sandy beaches, lush green hillsides dotted with houses of brilliant purple, orange, scarlet and electric blue – and dunes everywhere.

Our exploration of the islands is aided by Frank Delaney, a longtime family friend. He takes us to see my in-law's first home. The house is painted a soft peach with blue trim and it has a full veranda. We continue north to the island of Grande-Entrée. The harbour is filled with fishing boats – not surprising as fishing is an integral part of the economy. At the church graveyard, Tony is moved at the sight of Louis D'Amour's grave. He and Ludger reflect on their grandfather as a young boy, as a sea captain, as an islander.

On to Havre-Aubert and a stop at the Artisans du Sable, where artists add a secret resin developed on the islands to solidify the sand, then they sculpt the block into beautiful creations, ranging in colour from cream to charcoal, depicting all the natural colours of the island's sand.

La Grave on Havre-Aubert is a stretch of small shops and studios where local painters, sculptors and woodcarvers create art before your eyes. The Café de la Grave has an ambiance never forgotten – plus the best meat pie I've ever tasted. In the old beamed building, the owner plays the piano; other diners take turns at the keys while young people play chess.

We visit the Musée de la Mer and pick up a map recording the hundreds of shipwrecks that have occurred off the Maggies.

Later, we meet Octave Turbide, 90, who knew grandfather as Uncle Louis. He tells us more about this man he was so close to. He says Louis used phrases and sang songs new to the islanders. He tells us about Louis' first wife who died when Tony's father was five years old. He remarried a strange woman, according to Octave. When Louis was assisting at a funeral, one of the ropes lowering the coffin into the grave became entangled and Louis jumped into the grave to free it. When he told his wife what had happened, she was horrified. She was sure he would be the next one in the grave on the islands. And he was. At 63, he took sick and died.

On our final evening, Tony's cousin, Gilles Arseneault, takes us for a boat tour of l'Île d'Entrée. As we head west to Havre-Aubert, he points out Sandy Hook, the spot where Louis and his men clung to their boat and fought to stay alive against the vicious winter winds.

On this calm warm evening, it's almost impossible to imagine what Louis and his crew must have endured, but it's clear to all of us why he chose to stay.

Antonio D'Amour

Antonio D'Amour lives in Nova Scotia. The 15th of a family of seventeen, he has, over the years, collected and researched stories and anecdotes related to family history.

His wife, **Donna D'Amour**, is also a writer. The team offers dynamic workshops on writing family histories.

For more information visit our website at
www. zenobipublishing.ca
or
email: antonio@ns.sympatico.ca